Golden Bells
Daily Devotional
Volume 1

Copyright information

Unless otherwise stated, scripture references are taken from The Holy Bible, New International Version® NIV® Copyright © 1973, 1978, 1984, 2011 by Biblica, Inc. Used with permission. All rights reserved worldwide. (Note: This version does not capitalize the personal pronouns when referring to deity.)

Scripture references marked NKJV are taken from the New King James Version®. Copyright © 1982 by Thomas Nelson. Used by permission. All rights reserved. Scripture references marked KJV and RV are taken from the King James Version (1611) and the Revised Version (1881/85) respectively, both of which are in the Public Domain.

Golden Bells is published by:
Hayes Press,
c/o The Barn, Flaxlands,
Royal Wootton Bassett,
Swindon, Wiltshire UK
SN4 8DY.

e: info@hayespress.org
w: www.hayespress.org

Every effort is made to identify and ascribe copyright where applicable, but please do contact us if you wish to discuss permissions.

Welcome to Golden Bells Volume 1

Golden Bells has been feeding Christians around the world with God's word for a number of decades in a tear-off calendar format. In this first undated volume, each 7 days cycle through one of seven different approaches to enjoying God's Word:

1. An encouraging word to get us thinking about mission; whether that's evangelism or other service for the Lord;
2. A quote or an anecdote to enjoy and share;
3. A study or meditation about a particular Bible word or phrase;
4. Food for thought about God's word or our disciple lives;
5. Poetry or prose to meditate upon;
6. A motivational challenge;
7. A warm thought to stimulate our hearts and minds for worship.

The 'Daily Reading' passages aim to cover around 30 verses per day. Following this system of reading fully would take you through the whole Bible in just over 3½ years.

Day 1

...from the beginning of the year to its end.
(Deuteronomy 11:12)

Daily reading: Mark 3

I want the New Year's opening days
To fill with love, and prayer, and praise,
Some little thing to do for You,
For You have done great things for me.
I want some other soul to bring to You,
My Saviour and my King.
You will not, Lord, my prayer deny,
For You can all my wants supply.
In Jesus' Name our prayer we raise,
Whose guiding hand has blessed our days.
And may we, Lord, in godly fear
Serve You through all this coming year.
(Author unknown)

Day 2

Cast your cares on the Lord and he will sustain you.
(Psalm 55:22)

Daily reading: Mark 4:1-20

The cart driver drew alongside a lad who was struggling with a heavy pack. 'Like a lift?' he asked. He sat beside the driver with a sigh of relief but he kept the load on his back. 'Why don't you put your pack down?' 'Well, it's good enough of you to give me a lift,' he replied, 'without your horse having to carry my load as well.' Simplistic? Maybe, but isn't it true we often bring our burden to the Lord and then we continue to carry it ourselves?

Cast on Him thine every burden, whatso'er it be;
Hear His voice unto thee saying, 'Cast thy care on Me.'
(Isobel Hickling)

Day 3

'Lord,' Martha said to Jesus. (John 11:21)
'Yes, Lord,' she replied. (John 11:27)
'But, Lord,' said Martha... (John 11:39)

Martha teaches us how to address the Saviour. Three times in John 11 she calls Him 'Lord.' In verse 28 of the same chapter, she refers to Him as 'Master': 'The Master is come' (KJV). As disciples, we follow the example given in Luke 24:3 where He is called 'the Lord Jesus.' Peter talks about 'our Lord Jesus Christ' (2 Pet.1:8). Often in the gospels and in the book of Hebrews he is simply called 'Jesus' and these references are very sweet. But, like Martha, it's good and right that we call Him 'Lord.'

> I am trusting Thee for power, Thine can never fail;
> Words which Thou Thyself shalt give me must prevail.
> I am trusting Thee, Lord Jesus, never let me fall;
> I am trusting Thee for ever and for all.
> (Frances Ridley Havergal)

Day 4

Can both fresh water and salt water flow from the same spring? (James 3:11)

Daily reading: Mark 5:1-20

If you're a tea drinker, do you agree it tastes better out of a china cup? Do you use particular cups for tea or warm the teapot before brewing? Do you insist that the milk, if any, is poured into the cup before the tea? Would you use the same pot to brew both tea and coffee? Perish the thought! If we can be precise in such relatively minor things, then we should try to keep the more important parts of our lives in proper order. When Jesus was here, He had to condemn those who made a ritual out of cleaning the outside of their cups but forgot about the inside. His lesson wasn't about dishwashing, of course! He was pointing out how we must be in a clean condition for God to use – and He looks at the heart, not just how we appear to others.

> Lord, speak to me that I may speak
> In living echoes of your tone.
> As Thou hast sought, so let me seek
> Thine erring children, lost and lone.
> Oh, fill me with Thy fullness, Lord,
> Until my very hearts o'erflows
> In kindling thought and glowing word,
> Thy love to tell, Thy praise to show.
> (Frances Ridley Havergal)

Day 5

Will not the Judge of all the earth do right? (Genesis 18:25)

Daily reading: Mark 5:21-43

As the sea threatened Peter with drowning, his cry for help met with an instant response. As sickness threatened their brother with death, Mary and Martha's cry for help met with two days' delay. Whether the Lord's help is prompt or postponed, His motives are the same. He is 'righteous in all his ways and faithful in all he does' (Ps.145:17).

> The mightiest hand that ever moved could wait to bring relief;
> "Two days'" apparent heedlessness of nature's deepest grief.
> Would they have missed that sacred thing,
> His sympathy, His tears, scene on which breaking hearts
> Have leaned o'er nineteen hundred years?
> Oh, heart that loves so perfectly! Thou often waitest still,
> And blessed are the empty hearts Thy sympathy can fill.
> (Dora Rowan)

Day 6

… why did you steal my gods? … But if you find anyone who has your gods, that person shall not live. (Genesis 31:30,32)

Daily reading: Mark 6:1-29

Idols can provoke deep emotions, can't they? When Laban caught up with Jacob at Gilead, it was the accusation of having stolen his household gods that stirred the most bitter response from Jacob. Though the truth was unknown to Jacob, Rachel had touched Laban's most tender spot by stealing his gods. Is there something 'untouchable' hidden away in your life, something that you'd fiercely defend although it shouldn't be there?

> The dearest idol I have known, whate'er that idol be,
> Help me to tear it from its throne, and worship only Thee.
> So shall my walk be close with God,
> Calm and serene my frame;
> So purer light shall mark the road
> That leads me to the Lamb.
> (William Cowper)

Day 7

"I am," said Jesus. "And you will see the Son of Man sitting at the right hand of the Mighty One and coming on the clouds of heaven." The high priest tore his clothes … (Mark 14:62-63)

Daily reading: Mark 6:31-56

When Moses saw the glory of the great "I AM", he bowed his head and worshipped (Ex.34:8). Yet, when the Lord Jesus uttered those immortal words, we can imagine Caiaphas, with head lifted in arrogance, as he accused Him of blasphemy. Have you ever wondered what the angels thought as they saw the One whom they adored being so accused then condemned to be worthy of death, spit upon, whipped, His prophecy mocked and received with the blows of men's hands? A long way from the shameful dealings of the temple court that night, we bow our heads in the presence of Christ the Lord, the great "I AM".

Day 8

"Are you the only one visiting Jerusalem who does not know the things that have happened there in these days?" (Luke 24:18)

Daily reading: Mark 7

Cleopas just couldn't believe it. How could anyone possibly be ignorant of the front-page news in Jerusalem about the sudden death of Jesus of Nazareth? But Cleopas wouldn't have anybody not knowing about Jesus - He would soon put the stranger in the picture! We bump into many people today who haven't got a clue about what really happened in Jerusalem 2,000 years ago. Are we as quick to tell the news about Jesus as Cleopas was? Or, because of fear, do we let people pass us by without telling them something about Him? It was a scary time for the disciples, but Cleopas risked his life to take the opportunity. Let's take our opportunities as well.

Day 9

Be on your guard; stand firm in the faith. (1 Corinthians 16:13) So, if you think you are standing firm, be careful that you don't fall! (1 Corinthians 10:12)

Daily reading: Mark 8

The story's told of a man who was experienced in the sailing of small boats. He asked a friend what he thought would be the greatest hazard a sailor in a small boat had to face. 'Storms?' guessed his friend. 'No,' replied the sailor. 'In a storm, you'd hold fast to something when you were on deck. But in calm weather you might walk the deck without taking precautions and even a little roll of the boat could throw you into the sea. Calm and fair weather can be the most dangerous!' Let's be careful when life's voyage seems easy that we don't relax our watchfulness against the evil one – we always need to stay well within touching distance of our Lord!

> Will your anchor hold in the storms of life,
> When the clouds unfold their wings of strife?
> When the strong tides lift, and the cables strain,
> Will your anchor drift, or firm remain?
> We have an anchor that keeps the soul
> Steadfast and sure while the billows roll;
> Fastened to the Rock which cannot move,
> Grounded firm and deep in the Saviour's love!
> (Priscilla J. Owens)

Day 10

**Cast but a glance at riches, and they are gone, for they will surely sprout wings and fly off to the sky like an eagle.
(Proverbs 23:5)**

Daily reading: Mark 9:1-29

What are you focusing on? Isn't it most likely that you'll set your eyes where you've set your affections (Col.3:2)? Strangely enough, the word for 'set' in the Hebrew language is exactly the same as the word for 'fly.' So the message is clear: don't be flighty! It's short-sighted and will bring spiritual glaucoma. In the increasingly hazy vision, without you even noticing, worldly wealth sprouts wings and disappears. What a loss: there'll be no profit now and, in the future, no praise either.

Then I would set my heart to find inward adornings of the mind, knowledge and virtue, truth and grace, my richest robes before His face. It never fades, it ne'er grows old, nor fears the rain, nor moth, nor mould; it takes no spot, but still refines; the more 'tis worn, the more it shines. (Isaac Watts)

Day 11

Wounds from a friend can be trusted, but an enemy multiplies kisses. (Proverbs 27:6)

Daily reading: Mark 9:30-50

Do you ever challenge the way your friends speak or behave? If you don't, it definitely can't be because they never say or do anything the Lord would disapprove of! The reality is it's far easier to gossip behind someone's back or pretend to look the other way than risk a sharp answer or an accusation of hypocrisy.   But we're actually betraying our friends by pretending that everything's OK while they go on sinning. We can make excuses about not knowing the right words, but if we're prayerfully before the Lord about it then His grace is enough in all circumstances to help us speak the truth in love. Where would David have been without Nathan (2 Sam.12), Peter without the Lord (Jn 21), or Peter without Paul? (Gal.2:11) – and where might your friend end up without you?

Day 12

... the Lord disciplines the one he loves. (Hebrews 12:6) Blessed is the one whom God corrects. (Job 5:17)

Daily reading: Mark 10:1-22

It's interesting to watch a sheep dog rounding up the sheep into the pen. They try to stray but are quickly brought to where they should be. They eventually learn that to go in the direction the sheep dog wants is best for them, even if it seems restrictive at first. If only we had at least that much awareness of the Lord's direction in our lives!

Pressed into knowing no helper but God;
Pressed into loving the staff and the rod.
Pressed into liberty where nothing clings;
Pressed into faith for impossible things.
Pressed into living a life for the Lord,
Pressed into living a Christ-life outpoured.
(Annie Johnson Flint)

Day 13

A very large crowd spread their cloaks on the road, while others cut branches from the trees and spread them on the road. (Matthew 21:8)

Daily reading: Mark 10:23-52

When a player scores a 'hat-trick' (of goals or 'home runs') during a North American sport, many in the crowd will throw their caps onto the playing surface in tribute, taking the risk that they likely won't get them back! Many hundreds of clothes strewn on the road to Jerusalem amongst the branches made recovery just as challenging, never mind the fact they'd been walked over firstly by a donkey, then by the disciples and probably trampled by hundreds of other folks' feet. If the item was new, it would never be the same again. If you and I had been there, would we have been willing to take off our 'finery' and sacrifice it to Him? In all that we are, is there a part of our lives that we find difficult to lay down before Him?

Sinners, whose love can ne'er forget the wormwood and the gall,
Go, spread your trophies at His feet. and crown Him, crown Him Lord of all!
(Edward Perronet)

Day 14

Therefore, brothers and sisters, since we have confidence to enter the Most Holy Place by the blood of Jesus ... let us draw near to God with a sincere heart and with the full assurance that faith brings ... (Hebrews 10:19,22)

Daily reading: Mark 11

When we break bread each week, we tread that 'newly slain' way from where the Lord was on the tree to where He is on the throne. As God's people enter in, the sacrifice is seen as slain immediately prior to their entrance; it's as though the victim has been freshly killed. From His past, the dying Lamb has opened up the living way. What a present joy is ours as we are present! Having 'boldness (RV)' – a present confidence. Having 'a High Priest' – a present experience. Having assurance ... 'Let us draw near' – a present entrance.

The gate is open wide, the new and living way
Is clear and free and bright with love and peace and day!
Into the Holies now we come – our present and eternal home.
Enthroned in majesty the great Priest sits within,

The precious blood once shed has made and keeps us clean.
With boldness let us now draw near - that blood has banished every fear!
(Horatius Bonar)

Day 15

Answer me, Lord, out of the goodness of your love; in your great mercy turn to me. (Psalm 69:16)

Daily reading: Mark 12:1-27

Yesterday, we walked upward on the living way. Today, we walk outward to dying men. Does the afterglow of His presence go with us? It will if we live in the goodness of His lovingkindness. By it, He drew us from our past need to Himself; by it, He will turn to face us in our present need. Like David, we say, "Because your love is better than life, my lips will glorify you. I will praise you as long as I live" (Ps.63:2-3). He draws. He turns. We praise.

Draw me to You, till far within Your rest,
In stillness of Your peace, Your voice I hear;
For ever quieted upon Your breast, So loved, so near.
(Gerhard Tersteegen)

Day 16

I will rejoice in the Lord, I will be joyful in God my Saviour. (Habakkuk 3:18)

Daily reading: Mark 12:28-44

After a lot of effort, a group of prospectors found gold but kept their success secret. Soon afterwards, they visited a nearby town to buy food and were amazed when people congratulated them on their find. 'How did you know about it?' they asked. 'We haven't told anyone!' 'We could tell just by the look on your faces!' came the answer. On the other hand, a man was preaching in the open air and he challenged one of the crowd, who was a Christian, 'Are you saved?' 'Yes, of course I am,' came the terse reply. 'Then I suggest that as soon as possible you tell your face about it!' Ouch! We have much to shout about and to rejoice and be glad in as believers in Christ. But even if we say nothing, let's show to others by our faces what Christ means to us – and that we've found Someone more precious than gold!

Oh, the unsearchable riches of Christ! Wealth that can never be told;
Riches exhaustless of mercy and grace, precious, more precious than gold!
Precious, more precious, wealth that can never be told!

Oh, the unsearchable riches of Christ! Precious, more precious than gold!
(Fanny Crosby)

Day 17

You shall eat in plenty and be satisfied, and praise the name of the Lord your God, Who has dealt wondrously with you ... (Joel 2:23,26 NKJV)

Daily reading: Mark 13

'Wondrous' is an exceptional Bible word. It always, and only, refers to works done by God. "He only doeth wondrous things" (Ps.72:18 KJV). Samson's parents were face to face with the One Who fulfilled His Name (Judg.13:19 NKJV). He is Wonderful (Is.9:6) and He did wondrously. And now, because of Him, those who are wonderfully saved can respond to the call of the psalmist: "Sing to Him, sing psalms to Him; Talk of all His wondrous works!" (Ps.105:2 NKJV).

O what wondrous, wondrous love
Brought me down at Jesus' feet!
O such wondrous, dying love
Asks a sacrifice complete!
(Sarah Jean Graham)

Day 18

Take another scroll and write on it all the words that were on the first scroll, which Jehoiakim king of Judah burned up. (Jeremiah 36:28)

Daily reading: Mark 14:1-25

Jehoiakim was a wicked king of Judah and when the Lord warned him of the judgement that was going to fall on him he tore up the scroll on which Jeremiah had recorded the Lord's words and burned it in the fire. The amazing thing about our verse is that God told Jeremiah to write exactly the same words on another scroll and take it to the king. How merciful our God is! Instead of coming swiftly upon such a reckless act in judgement, He gives Jehoiakim another opportunity to read, learn and obey. Likewise, He Himself wrote out the 10 Commandments a second time for His people to obey. We must all be so thankful that our God is still like this – a God of second chances. 'To You, O Lord, belongs mercy' (Ps.62:12).

See mercy, mercy from on high
Descend to rebels doomed to die;
'Tis mercy free, which knows no bound;
How grand, how gladsome is the sound!
It triumphed when from death He rose
And brake the power of all His foes;
And since He took His seat on high
Now mercy reigns eternally!
(Robert Sandeman)

Day 19

Let us run with endurance the race that is set before us, looking unto Jesus ... (Hebrews 12:2-3 NKJV)

Daily reading: Mark 14:26-49

If the trials of your way, and the burdens of the day,
Cause your heart to feel dismay – Look to Him!
If to weariness inclined, and are fainting in your mind,
Then this heaven-sent answer find – Look to Him!
Look above and not within, why be overcome with sin?
He has conquered every struggle – Look to Him!
Every trial, every fear, every heartache, every tear:
Even now, He's drawing near – Look to Him!
(Author unknown)

Day 20

Whoever believes in me, as Scripture has said, rivers of living water will flow from within them. (John 7:38)

Daily reading: Mark 14:50-72

We don't think twice about putting our hands under the tap to let the stream of water clean them or our bodies under the shower to refresh us. We might think water's a gentle, light substance, but when it's driven by strong winds it can easily demolish houses by the shore, as the Lord pointed out in His parable of the house built on the sand. In our text, Jesus likens the Spirit of God to flowing water – that reminds us of the purification that the Spirit wants to cause in our lives, and the refreshment He wants to bring, but it also reminds us of His all-powerfulness as God the Holy Spirit. Stephen accused some of daring to resist the Holy Spirit, not just as a one-off but repeatedly (Acts 7:51). How did they do it? By consistently failing to recognize and obey the revealed word of God - are we guilty of making a similar mistake?

How I praise Thee, precious Savior,
That Thy love laid hold of me;
Thou hast saved and cleansed and filled me
That I might Thy channel be.
Jesus, fill now with Thy Spirit
Hearts that full surrender know;
That the streams of living water
From our inner self may flow.
(Mary E. Maxwell)

Day 21

Know that the Lord is God. It is he who made us, and we are his; we are his people, the sheep of his pasture. Enter his gates with thanksgiving and his courts with praise; give thanks to him and praise his name. (Psalm 100:3-4)

Daily reading: Mark 15:1-20

The scriptural order for us to keep the Lord's command to remember Him is in three steps: examine … enter … eat. The self-examination is centred around three passages: 1 Corinthians 11:28, Matthew 5:23,24 and Matthew 18:15-17. The purpose of entering into the Lord's presence has three elements: thanksgiving, praise and blessing. Is your heart ready and overflowing to participate in all three for these three things - who God is, what He's done for us and who He has made us?

Holy, holy, holy, we now come before Thee,
Gathered in that holy name so very dear to Thee,
O Lord God, we own Thee, humbly we adore Thee,
For Thy grace and power and truth and love we see.
Holy, holy, holy, humbly we adore Thee,
Honour, blessing, power and might, we would ascribe to Thee;
Courts of heaven ringing with the praise we're bringing,
For the One who lives our living Lord to be.
(G.T. Reeve)

Day 22

I believe God. (Acts 27:25 NKJV)

Daily reading: Mark 15:21-47

Just three simple words, but it's an excellent summary of Paul's faith. His strong affirmation of it must have rang out above the noise of the storm and his calmness must have been a real contrast to the panic setting in for the others on board. "So keep up your courage [take heart, cheer up], men, for I have faith in God that it will happen just as he told me." And they did take heart; and it did cheer them up. Even those who don't believe in God themselves are impressed by the faith of those who do. Let's remember that others are watching us. Our faith makes its impact upon unbelievers and fellow-Christians alike. So let's show by our lives and our lips where our confidence lies. God didn't let Paul down, and He won't let us down either.

I know not why God's wondrous grace to me has been made known
Nor why, unworthy as I am, He claimed me for his own.
But "I know whom I have believed, and am persuaded that he is able
To keep that which I've committed unto him against that day."
(D.W. Whittle)

Day 23

**Religion that God our Father accepts as pure and faultless is this…to keep oneself from being polluted by the world.
(James 1:27)**

Daily reading: Mark 16

The Lot who went into Sodom was barely recognisable as the Lot who came out (Gen.19:1-38). A young Christian girl strongly defended her attendance at some questionable places of amusement, insisting that a Christian could go anywhere. "Oh, she can," agreed her companion, "but I remember a friend going in a white dress to explore a coal mine. When others in the group questioned the wisdom of doing so, she appealed to the old miner-guide, "Can't I wear a white dress in the mine?" "There's nothing to keep you from wearing it down, but there's plenty to keep you from wearing it back," came the wise reply. Christian, mind where you go today.

O let me feel Thee near me, the world is ever near;
I see the sights that dazzle, the tempting sounds I hear;
My foes are ever near me, around me and within;
Lord Jesus, draw Thou nearer, and shield my soul from sin.
(J.E. Bude)

Day 24

Come to me, all you who are weary and burdened, and I will give you rest. Take my yoke upon you and learn from me, for I am gentle and humble in heart, and you will find rest for your souls. (Matthew 11:28-29)

Daily reading: Ezekiel 1

These verses supply the secret of spiritual success and the power for progress. 'Come' indicates revelation, 'yoke' indicates relationship and 'burden' indicates responsibility. 'Come' speaks of revelation expressed. 'Take' speaks of revelation experienced. 'Learn' speaks of revelation explored and 'Find' speaks of revelation exhibited. What great truths lie here in the only New Testament verse which speaks of the heart of the Lord Jesus Christ.

> O Lord, with sorrow, and with shame, we meekly would confess,
> How little we, who bear Thy name,Thy mind, Thy will, express.
> Give us Thy meek, Thy lowly mind; We fain would like Thee be;
> And all our rest and pleasure find in learning, Lord, of Thee.
> (James G. Deck)

Day 25

The man of God came up and told the king of Israel, "This is what the Lord says: 'Because the Arameans think the Lord is a god of the hills and not a god of the valleys, I will deliver this vast army into your hands, and you will know that I am the Lord.'" (1 Kings 20:28)

Daily reading: Ezekiel 2

The Syrians made the foolish mistake of thinking God was one-dimensional like their deities. They'd somehow got the idea that God's power was limited to the hills and not available in the valleys. Moses, Elijah, Peter, James and John could all testify to the exhilaration of mountain-top experiences with God, where his power was clearly on display. The greatest display of God's power was on the hill of Calvary. It was a valley experience for the Lord and, in His wisdom, God sends valley experiences to us also - but, praise His Name, it's there that He supplies the refreshing springs of His Word and His presence.

Day 26

God, who is rich in mercy, made us alive with Christ ... it is by grace you have been saved. And God raised us up with Christ and seated us with him in the heavenly realms in Christ Jesus, in order that in the coming ages he might show the incomparable riches of his grace ... (Ephesians 2:4-7)

Daily reading: Ezekiel 3

In Ephesians 1:7 we see the saving riches of God's grace shown to us now. In Ephesians 2:7 we see the surpassing riches of His grace to be shown to us in eternity. Isn't that wonderful? The day of grace will end, but grace goes on forever!

"Whilst in this place secure my soul shall rest, Throughout eternal ages I shall be, The object of the boundless love of God, When in surpassing kindness He will show, To me th'exceeding riches of His grace In blissful, peaceful rest, before His face." (Author unknown)

Day 27

... he sent the people to their homes, joyful and glad in heart for the good things the Lord had done for David and Solomon and for his people Israel. (2 Chronicles 7:10)

Daily reading: Ezekiel 4

Home life is the real barometer of the state of God's people. Spiritual condition cannot be concealed there. We may try, like Achan, to hide our ungodliness there (Josh.7) but ultimately it will be exposed. Like Israel, we may have ill-spent hours of murmuring there, but that only exposes a rebellious spirit. Our homes should be places from which we emerge in the enjoyment of God and to which we return with increased joy, after times of fellowship with His people in His service. But are they?

O happy home, where Thou art loved the dearest,
Thou loving Friend, and Saviour of our race,
And where among the guests there never cometh
One who can hold such high and honored place!
(Karl Johann Philipp Spitta)

Day 28

Therefore, when Christ came into the world, he said: "Sacrifice and offering you did not desire, but a body you prepared for me. (Hebrews 10:5)

Daily reading: Ezekiel 5

What a stupendous contemplation, the brightness of God's glory, the express image of His substance. Heir of all things, Maker of the worlds and their Upholder, here on earth to take the *body* prepared for Him through the overshadowing of the Highest. Early in His public ministry, the Lord alluded to the destruction of that *body* (Jn 2:19). To the indignation of Judas, the woman lavished expensive ointment on His *body*. Most staggering of all, He "bore our sins in His *body* on the cross" (1 Pet.2:24).

> The loaf he took spoke of that frame
> Prepared by God for Him who came
> To manifest His Father's name, Jesus, our Lord.
> How solemn is the broken bread! Sign of His holy body, dead.
> Who suffered in our room and stead, Jesus, our Lord.
> (Charles Mann Luxmoore)

Day 29

Lord, you have been our dwelling place throughout all generations. Before the mountains were born or you brought forth the whole world, from everlasting to everlasting you are God. (Psalm 90:1-2)

Daily reading: Ezekiel 6

All his life, he'd been confined to the Californian mountains. Will was impressed by the wonders of life in San Francisco, but what astounded him most was the vastness of the Pacific Ocean. Returning to its shore on his final day, he filled his screw-top jar from the ocean because he was "gonna take it back and make them believe" – a pint of water to convey to his people the staggering extent of the earth's largest ocean! Will would learn that they ultimately had to go and experience it for themselves, but it was a start. What 'pint of water' can you use today to get someone started on the greatest journey of discovery they will ever take – to experience the eternal, all-powerful, all-knowing, all-loving God?

Jehovah reigns, He dwells in light, girded with majesty and might,
The world created by His hands, firm on its first foundation stands.
But ere this spacious world was made, or had its first foundation laid,
Thy throne eternal ages stood, Thyself the ever-living God.
(Isaac Watts)

Day 30

So, as the Holy Spirit says: "Today, if you hear his voice, do not harden your hearts as you did in the rebellion, during the time of testing in the wilderness ..." (Hebrews 3:7-8)

Daily reading: Ezekiel 7

Portius Festus, a Roman governor, was either a very busy man or a procrastinator. Three times we read in Acts 25 of 'tomorrow.' But in Hebrews, three times we read of "Today". As Martin Luther King said, "We are now faced with the fact that tomorrow is today. We are confronted with the fierce urgency of now." We must never be too busy to hear and obey the voice of the Lord. Who are we to say 'tomorrow' when He has said 'today'? Away with hearts hardened by the busyness of the world or by sheer laziness and let's present ourselves in obedience to the Lord TODAY.

This is the day the Lord has made
In it He has his grace displayed
'Tis ours to sing in holy lays
For all His love, our grateful praise.
The future, Lord, we do not know,
But seek that we in grace may grow.
To meet what comes in simple faith,
Believing what the Scripture saith.
(Charles Mann Luxmoore)

Day 31

**...joint-heirs with Christ; if so be that we suffer with him, that we may be also glorified together. For I reckon that the sufferings of this present time are not worthy to be compared with the glory which shall be revealed in us.
(Romans 8:17-18 KJV)**

This isn't wishful guesswork, but a reasoned and logical conclusion. That's the meaning of 'reckon', and such an analysis comes from the man who was shown in advance "how <u>many</u> things he must suffer for My Name's sake." When he calculates the sufferings of time with the glories of eternity, he's not in any doubt it's worth it. James Deck agrees:

> A little while, 'twill soon be past!
> Why should we shun the shame and cross?
> Oh, let us in His footsteps haste
> And count for Him all else but loss:
> Oh, how will recompense His smile,
> The sufferings of this little while!
> (J.G. Deck)

Day 32

But avoid foolish controversies and genealogies and arguments and quarrels about the law because these are unprofitable and useless. (Titus 3:9)

Daily reading: Ezekiel 9

"Did Jesus own the clothes He wore?" might not be a question you've spent much time considering; believe it or not, it's a question debated furiously by two orders of monks in a famous novel by Umberto Eco. The important principles behind the debate had been lost a long time ago and all that remained was a trivial argument in which detail was everything and winning was all that mattered. There are two extremes in the search for knowledge. One says that a matter's too difficult, so I won't bother, but the other pursues it whatever the cost. Neither is glorifying to God. Knowledge comes from God and if we need knowledge for His service then we should pursue it. If not, we'll be far better off dropping it.

Day 33

I prayed for this child, and the Lord has granted me what I asked of him. So now I give him to the Lord. For his whole life he will be given over to the Lord. (1 Samuel 1:27-28)

Daily reading: Ezekiel 10

For what is the Lord asking you today? Whatever it is, it's only on loan! He'll repay! Can you refuse?

Peter lent a boat to save Him from the press;
Martha lent a home, with busy kindliness.
One man lent a colt, another lent a room;
Some threw down their clothes, and Joseph lent a tomb.
Simon lent his strength the cruel cross to bear;
Mary spices brought His body to prepare.
But what have I to lend – no boat, no house, no lands.
Dwell, Lord, in my heart and use these feeble hands.
(Author unknown)

Day 34

"A new command I give you: Love one another. As I have loved you, so you must love one another. By this everyone will know that you are my disciples, if you love one another." (John 13:34,35)

Daily reading: Ezekiel 11

Along with the new birth, new creation, new man, new name, new song, and a new and living way, is a new commandment. It's the all-important request of the Lord that we love one another. By doing it, others will know that He loves us and that we're His disciples. The love request flows from Calvary, the place where His love was fully expressed, even to those who had no love for Him – like Judas, whose only love was for money and left the Upper Room to betray the Lord just seconds before the commandment was given. It's often said that actions speak louder than words, but words that are spoken genuinely can have as dramatic an effect. Will you prove it today by saying to your brothers or sisters in Christ, "I love you!"?

What grace, O Lord, and beauty shone around Thy steps below!
What patient love was seen in all Thy life of death and woe!
Oh, give us hearts to love like Thee, like Thee, O Lord, to grieve
Far more for others' sins, than all the wrongs that we receive.
One with Thyself, may every eye, in us, Thy brethren see,
That gentleness and grace that spring from union, Lord, with Thee.
(Sir Edward Denny)

Day 35

My God, my God, why have you forsaken me? Why are you so far from saving me, so far from my cries of anguish? (Psalm 22:1)

Daily reading: Ezekiel 12

Both Hosea and Amos said that God roars like a lion. But what about His Son? Deep within the night season of the cross, when darkness hid Him from those who looked at Him like "a ravening and a roaring lion," (Ps.22:13 KJV) He roared. There were long agonized rumblings of His spirit and intense moanings of His soul. Like Job, He could have said, "My roarings are poured out like water" (Job 3:24 KJV). How uniquely solemn that the Lamb has roared.

A man of sorrows once He was,
No friend was found to plead his cause,
For all preferred the world's applause.
He groaned beneath sin's awful load.
For in the sinner's place He stood.
And died to bring us nigh to God.
But now He reigns with glory crowned,
And angel hosts the throne surround
And still His lofty praises sound.
(Thomas Kelly)

Day 36

Strengthen the feeble hands, steady the knees that give way; say to those with fearful hearts, "Be strong, do not fear ... he will come to save you." (Isaiah 35:3-4)

Daily reading: Ezekiel 13

When the fire broke out, a man yelled out in obvious alarm, "Don't panic! Stay calm!" The advice was good, but he was completely ignored as those who heard him did the exact opposite! Why? Because of the lack of confidence evident in his own voice. If we're successfully to point others to our strong Saviour, we've got to show simple but firm trust in Him.

I do not ask for mighty words to leave the crowd impressed,
But grant my life may ring so true my neighbour shall be blessed.
Though words of wisdom and of power come easily to some;
Give me this simple message, Lord, that bids the sinner come.
(Author unknown)

Day 37

Praise the Lord, my soul, and forget not all his benefits—who forgives all your sins … who redeems your life from the pit and crowns you with love and compassion, who satisfies your desires with good things so that your youth is renewed like the eagle's. (Psalm 103:2,4,5)

Daily reading: Ezekiel 14

How easy it is to forget the Lord's benefits and to grumble instead of being grateful. Mouths that He's satisfied with good things should magnify, not moan, and glorify, not grieve. When Matthew Henry was accosted by thieves and robbed of his purse, he wrote in his diary, "Let me be thankful first, because I was never robbed before; second, because although they took my purse, they did not take my life; third, because, although they took my all, it was not much; and fourth, because, it was I who was robbed, and not someone else." Is there anything you've forgotten to be thankful for today?

> Pardon for sin and a peace that endureth,
> Thine own dear presence to cheer and to guide.
> Strength for today and bright hope for tomorrow,
> Blessings all mine, with ten thousand besides.
> Great is Thy faithfulness! Great is Thy faithfulness!
> Morning by morning, new mercies I see,
> All I have needed Thy hand hath provided,
> Great is Thy faithfulness, Lord unto me.
> (T.O. Chisholm)

Day 38

As newborn babes, desire the pure milk of the word, that you may grow thereby. (1 Peter 2:2)
And the child Samuel grew in stature, and in favour both with the LORD and men. (1 Samuel 2:26)

Daily reading: Ezekiel 15

It's no surprise we read of a dedicated servant like Samuel that he growing (1 Sam.2:21;2:26;3:19). The word 'grew' means 'to twist' and like a row of weaving the effect of each day would be almost imperceptible; but we can imagine Hannah, having not seen Samuel for a year, saying to her husband after another annual visit, 'How he's grown!' The Lord shared their delight, for he grew not 'only in stature', but 'in favour ... with the LORD.' It must have been quite a lonely life for the lad, but his attention to the Lord's words and his careful obedience to the instruction of his mother and the old priest, Eli, ensured the disciplined training that was to mark him out (1 Sam.3:20) as an outstanding servant. Speaking spiritually, would anyone ever be able to say to you with delight, "How you've grown!"?

Day 39

For the eyes of the Lord range throughout the earth to strengthen those whose hearts are fully committed to him. (2 Chronicles 16:9)

Daily reading: Ezekiel 16:1-30

With their *special* pit organs, pythons can 'see' the heat of living bodies. Although its eyes are a *conventional* design, the goldfish don't only see near-infrared but also ultraviolet, which are both invisible to us. Swimming on the water's surface, the anableps' *bifocal* eyes enable it to see equally well above and below the surface. Amazing! But the Lord's eyes range over the whole earth – they are *global*. More than that, they see you as an *individual*. Perhaps, like Asa, you feel beleaguered by many forces today. Don't forget, as he did, that God isn't merely watching, but also waiting to reveal and provide His strength.

> There is an eye that never sleeps beneath the wings of night,
> There is an ear that never shuts when sink the beams of light.
> There is an arm that never tires when human strength gives way;
> There is a love that never fails when earthly loves decay.
> That eye is fixed on seraph thrones, that arm upholds the sky,
> That ear is filled with heavenly songs; that love is throned on high.
> But there's a power which faith can wield when mortal aid is vain,
> That eye, that arm, that love to reach, that listening ear to gain.
> That power is prayer which soars on high through Jesus on the throne
> And moves the hand which moves the world to bring deliverance down.
> (J.C. Wallace)

Day 40

Jesus replied, "You do not realize now what I am doing, but later you will understand." (John 13:7)

Fain would I roll aside the clouds to pierce the distant sky
Then soar away on eagle's wings, and into heaven fly:
Just for a moment there to gaze upon the Saviour's face;
To quickly bow and render thanks for all His love and grace.
But I must wait with patient hope, and view with eyes of faith,
Till dawns th'eternal morn when Christ will greet me face to face.
I know the glorious morn will come, I know the Sun will rise;
I know the beauties of that dawn will fill my wondering eyes.
(Author unknown)

Day 41

... this grace was given me: to preach to the Gentiles the boundless riches of Christ. (Ephesians 3:8)

Daily reading: Ezekiel 17

In 1886, Australian George Harrison stumbled across an outcrop of gold in the Transvaal of South Africa which turned out to be the world's greatest gold field. Credited with one of history's biggest understatements, Harrison said, "I think I have found a payable gold field" and wandered off, selling his claim for just £10! Many men have come close to discovering 'the boundless riches of Christ' yet they've wandered off – some with the same level of appreciation of the man who estimated the worth of those 'boundless riches' at just 30 pieces of silver, the price of a slave. Let us to whom Christ is precious beyond measure preach His 'boundless riches' to a world that's in the deepest spiritual poverty.

O Christ, in thee my soul hath found, and found in thee alone,
The peace, the joy I sought so long, the bliss till now unknown.
Now none but Christ can satisfy, none other name for me!
There's love and life and lasting joy, Christ Jesus, found in thee.
(Frances Bevan)

Day 42

...he will be raised and lifted up and highly exalted. Just as there were many who were appalled at him—his appearance was so disfigured beyond that of any human being and his form marred beyond human likeness ... (Isaiah 52:13-14)

Standing with John at Calvary, we marvel at the grace of our Lord Jesus, as we see His "appearance … disfigured beyond that of any human being", but, with John on Patmos, we marvel at the majestic might of our Lord Jesus as we see "His face … like the sun shining in all its brilliance" (Rev.1:16).

'Twas once for us all bruised and marred,
His brow with cruel thorn was scarred;
They nailed Him to the tree!
But then His face in glory bright
Shall fill our wondering, ravished sight,
And we like Him shall be.
(Charles Mann Luxmoore)

Day 43

For to me, to live is Christ, and to die is gain. (Philippians 1:21)

Daily reading: Ezekiel 19

He'd heard the good news of Jesus many times, but he'd rejected it. He'd even denied the existence of God and boasted that he was an atheist. Now his life was drawing to a close, and eternity opened before him. The philosopher Thomas Hobbes said to those near him, "I say again, if I had the whole world at my disposal, I would give it to live one day. I am about to take a leap into the dark." What a contrast to those who come to the end of their lives but have received the Saviour. No 'leap in the dark' for them! They depart to be with Christ, which is 'very far better.' In the meantime, let us who have this glorious hope remember our responsibility to those who die in darkness at our side. As Horatius Bonar urges:

Go, labour on while it is day;
The world's dark night is hastening on.
Speed, speed thy work, cast sloth away;
It is not thus that souls are won.
Men die in darkness at your side,
Without a hope to cheer the tomb,
Take up the torch and wave it wide,
The torch that light's time's thickest gloom.

Day 44

**We are hard pressed on every side, but not crushed;
perplexed, but not in despair; persecuted, but not
abandoned; struck down, but not destroyed.
(2 Corinthians 4:8-9)**

Daily reading: Ezekiel 20:1-32

Theodore Steinway, president of Steinway and Sons, once noted, "In one of our concert grand pianos, two hundred and forty-three taut strings exert a pull of forty thousand pounds on an iron frame. It is proof that out of great tension may come great harmony." When General Booth suffered blindness in old age, he said to his son, "Bramwell, I have sought to serve the Lord with my sight, now I must serve Him with my blindness." Time and again, melody has been sounded out of calamity, because men and women of God have known that whatever the adversity "the eternal God is your [their] refuge, and underneath are the everlasting arms" (Deut.33:27).

> What have I to dread, what have I to fear,
> Leaning on the everlasting arms?
> I have blessed peace with my Lord so near,
> Leaning on the everlasting arms.
> Leaning, leaning, safe and secure from all alarms;
> Leaning, leaning, leaning on the everlasting arms.
> (E.A. Hoffman)

Day 45

**And Hilkiah gave the book to Shaphan, and he read it ...
Shaphan read it before the king. (2 Kings 22:8-11)**

Daily reading: Ezekiel 20:33-49

The name of the king's scribe, Shaphan, comes from a root Hebrew word that means 'to conceal as a valuable, a treasure.' It's also the word for a coney, or rock-badger, so called because of its habit of hiding, and commended for its wisdom. Solomon, with his expert knowledge of animals (1 Kgs.4:33) commended the coney, which is also renowned for its continuous jaw action as it re-chews its food to aid digestion. Shaphan was true to his name, reading the book of the law himself, then reading it again before the king. It was like chewing it, then rechewing it! How do you treat **the** Book? Is it your constant 'meditation' (Ps.1:2), a word that carries the same thought of re-chewing? Does it gather dust or give delight? The choice is yours - you can either be wise (like the coney), or … otherwise!

Father of mercies, in Thy word what endless glory shines
Forever be Thy name adored for these celestial lines.
Oh, may the heavenly pages be our ever new delight,
And still new beauties may we see, and still increasing light.
Divine Instructor, gracious Lord, Thou art for ever near;
Teach us to love Thy sacred word and view the Saviour there.
(A. Steele)

Day 46

Whoever wants to be my disciple must deny themselves and take up their cross daily and follow me. (Luke 9:23)

Daily reading: Ezekiel 21

The Master will not ask of the disciple more than He gave Himself, so before He speaks of the cost of discipleship He reminds His faithful followers of the cost of Messiahship. He must "suffer many things and be rejected…and be killed." Self-denial and the denial of self are two different things. Self-denial can even lead to pride, but the denial of self is to take the lowest place in the highest interests of our God.

Higher than the highest heavens,
Deeper than the deepest sea,
Lord, Thy love at last hath conquered;
Grant me now my spirit's longing –
None of self, and all of Thee.
(Theodore Monod)

Day 47

Therefore we do not lose heart. Though outwardly we are wasting away, yet inwardly we are being renewed day by day. (2 Corinthians 4:16)

Daily reading: Ezekiel 22

How did you look this morning – spiritually? In the mirror of the Word are there signs of wear and tear? Are Christian qualities evident? They should be and can be!

There's a Man in the glory whose life is for me. He's pure and He's holy, triumphant and free; He's wise and He's loving, tender is He, And His life in the glory my life may be. His peace is abiding, patient is He. He's joyful and radiant, expecting to see His life in the glory lived out in me. (Mary E. McDonough)

Day 48

**He ... saw ... Jesus standing at the right hand of God.
(Acts 7:55)**

Daily reading: Ezekiel 23:1-35

Stephen wasn't the only person who saw Jesus that day. Saul, who guarded the clothes of the murderers, saw Him as well. He didn't see Him at the right hand of God, but in the face of the martyr. He was full of the Holy Spirit who did as the Lord foretold, "He will glorify Me" (Jn 16:14). In this Christ-glorifying death, Saul saw Jesus. You might not have to face violence and death, but whatever rains down on you today, will others see Jesus?

Not I, but Christ, be honored, loved, exalted;
Not I, but Christ, be seen, be known, be heard;
Not I, but Christ, in every look and action;
Not I, but Christ, in every thought and word.
Oh, to be saved from myself, dear Lord,
Oh, to be lost in Thee; Oh, that it may be no more I,
But Christ that lives in me.
(Ada Whiddington)

Day 49

Shout for joy to the Lord, all the earth. Worship the Lord with gladness; come before him with joyful songs. Enter his gates with thanksgiving and his courts with praise; give thanks to him and praise his name. (Psalm 100:1-2,4)

Daily reading: Ezekiel 23:36-49

Dr. W.H. Griffeth Thomas wrote, "There is joy in retrospect, as we look at the past; there is joy of aspect, as we look at the present; there is a joy of prospect, as we look forward to the future. There is the joy of memory, the joy of love, the joy of hope. There is the joy of the peaceful conscience, the joy of the grateful heart, the joy of the teachable mind, the joy of the trustful soul, the joy of the adoring spirit, the joy of the obedient life, and the joy of the glowing hope." Joyfully draw water from the wells of salvation today as you come into his gates with thanksgiving.

> Break forth and sing the song of glory to His name
> Wake every heart and every tongue to celebrate His fame.
> Sing of His dying love, His resurrection power;
> Sing how He intercedes above for those whose sins He bore.
> Sing on your heavenly road, ye heirs of glory, sing
> Of the ascended Christ of God your cheerful praises bring.
> (W. Hammond)

Day 50

David ... chose for himself five smooth stones from the brook ... and took out a stone; and he slung it and struck the Philistine. (1 Samuel 17:39,40,49)

Daily reading: 2 Corinthians 1

David would have used the same method to scare off, or perhaps even kill, wild animals that were savaging his sheep. Not any stone would do - it must be the right size, weight and shape. David knew by experience the type of stone he needed to put in his sling to bring down the mighty Goliath. God did the rest and directed it to perhaps the only area that would penetrate Goliath's defences. The Lord approached spiritual matters in different ways according to whom He was speaking; and Paul's preaching to the pagans in Athens was very different from his message in the synagogues of the Jews. We need to be wise servants, careful how we prepare the gospel message to gain the attention of the individual and allow the convicting Holy Spirit to take charge of the impact.

Day 51

The Lord has done great things for us, and we are filled with joy. (Psalm 126:3)

Daily reading: 2 Corinthians 2

"How are you keeping?" someone asked the ageing John Quincy Adams, an early president of the U.S.A. "Thank you," he replied, "John Quincy Adams is very well himself, sir, but the house in which he lives is falling to pieces. Times and seasons have nearly destroyed it. The roof is well-worn, the walls shattered and it trembles with every gale. I think John Quincy Adams will soon have to move out, but he himself is well, sir." Because of Calvary, all aged Christians can say with gladness, "The LORD has done great things for us" and also, "It is well with my soul."

Though Satan should buffet, though trials should come,
Let this blest assurance control:
That Christ has regarded my helpless estate,
And His blood has been shed for my soul.
It is well with my soul; it is well, it is well with my soul.
(Horatius Gates Spafford)

Day 52

He ... offered up prayers and supplications, with vehement cries and tears. (Hebrews 5:7)

Daily reading: 2 Corinthians 3

This is the only occurrence in the New Testament of the word translated 'supplications' here. It literally means 'olive-branch.' We still refer today to someone 'extending an olive branch' in a bid to make peace or avoid conflict, reflecting an actual custom that's thousands of years old. In the garden of Gethsemane – flat out on his face amid the olive branches – the Lord was asking if the conflict of Calvary could be avoided. There was to be no peace for Him, but He became our Peace (Eph.2:14).

The Son of God, the Prince of Life, thrice in the garden prayed
The sword was drawn to pierce the One on whom our sins were laid.
He asked, if it were possible, the cup might pass away;
Made flesh for us, the Son of God a prostrate suppliant lay.
Strong crying, tears and sweat like blood bespeak His agony,
Yet must He sink in deeper grief that we might never die.
(R.C. Chapman)

Day 53

Later that night, the boat was in the middle of the lake, and he was alone on land. He saw the disciples straining at the oars, because the wind was against them. Shortly before dawn he went out to them, walking on the lake. (Mark 6:47-48)

Daily reading: 2 Corinthians 4

What a blessing: the Lord sees what we feel. In His omniscience He sees and feels and understands everything that is contrary to us. When we put in the most energy and make the least progress, when we feel like saying, as Jacob did, "All these things are against me" (Gen.42:36), He draws near to be with us and for us. All we have to do is make room for Him in the boat!

> In all our troubles Jesus comes and whispers to us, "Peace."
> He sees us toiling as we row and bids the storm to cease.
> May we look up and see His face and may our faith increase.
> (Author unknown)

Day 54

If only they were wise and would understand this and discern what their end will be! (Deuteronomy 32:29)

Daily reading: 2 Corinthians 5

Do your days seem too long? Are troubles filling your thoughts, so that each moment drags on to prolong the gloom? If that's the case, it's good to switch our focus to where we're heading and take fresh courage from the Word of God for what are brief days of trial and opportunity in the grand scheme of eternity.

> Our life is long. Not so, wise angels say
> Who watch us waste it, trembling while they weigh
> Against eternity one squandered day.
> Our life is long. Not so the saints protest,
> Filled full of consolation and of rest:
> "Short ill, long good, one long unending best."
> (Christina Rossetti)

Day 55

The path of the righteous is like the morning sun, shining ever brighter till the full light of day. But the way of the wicked is like deep darkness; they do not know what makes them stumble. (Proverbs 4:18-19)

Daily reading: 2 Corinthians 6

In this dark world, it's very tempting for Christians to attempt to blend temporarily in with their surroundings like a chameleon to try and win acceptance by unbelievers. This animal, by the way, was marked out as unclean in the Levitical law (Lev.11:30). The Lord instructed the opposite; His disciples must let their lights – including the purity of their testimony - shine before men. The darker the ways of the world, the brighter we should stand out.   The word for chameleon in Leviticus 11 is translated as owl in other places. This ties in, too, because the owl is rarely in seen in broad daylight and swoops silently in the deep darkness. Will you blend in stealthily or shine brightly today?

> Walk in the light, so shalt thou know that fellowship of love,
> His Spirit only can bestow who reigns in light above.
> Walk in the light and thou shalt find the heart made truly His,
> Who dwells in cloudless light enshrined, in whom no darkness is.
> Walk in the light and thou shalt own Thy darkness passed away,
> Because that light hath on thee shone in which is perfect day.
> Walk in the light, thy path shall be steadfast, serene and bright,
> For God in grace shall dwell in thee, and God Himself is light.
> (B. Barton)

Day 56

For God was pleased to have all his fullness dwell in him, and through him to reconcile to himself all things, whether things on earth or things in heaven, by making peace through his blood, shed on the cross. (Colossians 1:19-20)

Daily reading: 2 Corinthians 7

We thank God for the two great pleasures He had in Christ. It pleased Him that all the fulness of the Godhead should reside bodily in His Son – what breadth there is in these words! Also, "it pleased the LORD to bruise Him" (Is.53:10 NKJV) in making His soul an offering for sin. What depth there is in these words! The pleasure in the second stems from the truth of the first. All the perfect attributes of God were in that lovely Man Who was despised and rejected of men and, as God manifested in the flesh, He alone had all the ability required to reconcile us to God. Hallelujah!

> The sword of God was bidden His holy one to smite,
> Jehovah's face was hidden in terrors from His sight,
> God's tokens had declared Him the Son who pleased Him well;
> He pierced His soul, nor spared Him, when bruised by earth and hell.
> His God who duly prized Him, whose statutes He did keep,
> In floods of death baptized Him in sorrow's lowest deep,
> He was the Father's treasure, the Christ whom He had sent,
> His righteous sore displeasure on Him for us was spent.
> (R.C. Chapman)

Day 57

My goal is that they may be encouraged in heart and united in love, so that they may have the full riches of complete understanding, in order that they may know the mystery of God, namely, Christ, in whom are hidden all the treasures of wisdom and knowledge. (Ephesians 2:2-3)

Daily reading: 2 Corinthians 8

A former Hindu was asked to explain what there was in Christianity that he had not found in Hinduism. He answered, "It was Christ!" "But what teaching or doctrine is there that is distinct from your former faith?" he was asked again. "It wasn't teaching or doctrine," he replied, "it was the living Christ!" "Perhaps I haven't made myself clear," the questioner objected. "What is different in Christianity from the philosophy of Hinduism which caused you to embrace Christianity?" "It was Christ," was still the answer. Not just a creed, doctrine or philosophy, but a transforming Christ! Is that your experience, too?

Day 58

For God so loved the world that He gave His only begotten Son, that whosoever believes in Him should not perish but have everlasting life. (John 3:16 NKJV)

Daily reading: 2 Corinthians 9

As the 'gospel in a nutshell', this verse is probably the most-quoted scripture from the entire Bible! There was a chuckle when a child mistakenly recited: 'God so loved the world that He gave His only *forgotten* Son ...' But there is more truth than fiction in the misquotation. Sadly, our beloved Saviour and Lord is often a forgotten Person. Incidentally, how many times have you thought about Him or mentioned His name today? He's worthy of our remembrance. He's done so much for us. He died that we might live with Him eternally. This alone deserves our frequent remembrance, followed by a fervent response.

Day 59

Woe to those who draw sin along with cords of deceit, and wickedness as with cart ropes ... (Isaiah 5:18)

This is the only place to find a cart rope in the Bible, and it describes the way of sin. The Jewish Talmud says, "A bad habit is first a caller, then a guest, and at last a master." Here in Isaiah, it is the same sequence. It begins with the flattering, delicate cords of vanity which we believe we can break as easily as a gossamer thread – just as easily as Samson broke Delilah's bowstrings. But the frail thread becomes more substantial until at last it's a cart rope that binds us. The cobwebs have become cables! Exercise spiritual discipline today, beware the silken cords, and break each habit that could result in your eternal loss.

Day 60

The king was distressed, but because of his oaths and his dinner guests, he ordered that her request be granted. (Matthew 14:9)

Daily reading: 2 Corinthians 11

The request referred to here was that the head of John the Baptist be presented on a platter. It was a heinous crime that king Herod commanded to be done and all in order to save face in front of his guests after previous careless words. Of course, he wasn't the only king to find himself in such a predicament – Darius was trapped into sending Daniel to what should have been a grisly fate in the lion's den. All of us figuratively put our feet in our mouths from time to time, however hard we try not to. However, when we make a mistake with our words we must ask God for the humility to admit we've got it wrong before it drags us deeper into trouble and we fall into the same trap as Herod.

Day 61

It always protects, always trusts, always hopes, always perseveres. Love never fails. (1 Corinthians 13:7-8)

Daily reading: 2 Corinthians 12

Our love often ebbs and flows like the tide. By comparison, this constant, selfless love is first of all seen in our blessed Lord Jesus and ought to be seen also in His disciples. Love is the badge of discipleship. To the question, 'What is love?', someone replied in poetry:

It's silence when your words would hurt,
It's patience when your neighbour's curt,
It's deafness when the scandal flows,
And blindness for another's woes;
It's promptness when stern duty calls
And courage when misfortune falls.
(Author unknown)

Day 62

**Here I am! I stand at the door and knock. If anyone hears my voice and opens the door, I will come in and eat with that person, and they with me.
(Revelation 3:20)**

Daily reading: 2 Corinthians 13

In Laodicea, they were unacceptably lukewarm, unsuspectingly poor, unknowingly blind and naked. Unintentionally, perhaps, they had locked out the Man of undying zeal, unknown wealth and unerring vision. Like a persistent merchant, He was knocking to offer them all that they needed – gold, clothes and eye salve - but also the exceptional privilege of eating with Him as their friend. C.S. Lewis suggested that one day it will be as if the door of hell is 'locked from the inside.' May that never be true of the door to our hearts – for what homeowner should need to knock to gain access?

At the door of my heart long the Saviour did stand,
And He knock'd many times with His nail-pierced hands;
But at last I gave ear, and I opened it wide,
And I asked Him to enter and with me abide.
Behold, at your door He doth stand and knock,
If any His voice will hear;
And, heeding the call, will their door unlock,
He'll enter and bless them there.
(Ada Habershon)

Day 63

Gideon went inside, prepared a young goat, and from an ephah of flour he made bread without yeast. (Judges 6:19)

It might have been a time of hardship and oppression, but Gideon made sure the LORD received a full portion – an ephah was equivalent to 10 omers, and an omer of manna had been enough to feed a person for a day (Ex.16:16). Gideon's bread was in fact ten times the specified amount and must have involved a lot of preparation and a lot of sacrifice! Let's ensure we are fully prepared to give to God a full portion in our worship.

> Baskets full of firstfruits, sacrifice of praise
> Songs of our Redeemer, joyfully we raise.
> Lord, we only offer but a thousandth part
> Of the love that's owed thee from each ransomed heart!
> Praise we now the Father, praise be to the Son,
> And the Holy Spirit; praise the Three in One.
> (J.B Belton)

Day 64

We, however, will not boast beyond proper limits, but will confine our boasting to the sphere of service God himself has assigned to us, a sphere that also includes you.
(2 Corinthians 10:13)

Daily reading: Joshua 2

The apostle Paul was an outstanding evangelist but that doesn't mean he wasn't very aware of divinely imposed limits. He wasn't at liberty to travel just where he pleased with the gospel, and neither can we rush in all directions at once. Just as God had once allocated the promised land between the various tribes of Israel, so Paul viewed allotted spheres or fields of service as being like lanes allocated to athletes at a race meeting. In making for the finishing line, athletes need to maintain lane discipline. Do we need a fresh sense of our divinely appointed sphere of evangelical service?

> Let none hear you idly saying, "There is nothing I can do,"
> While the souls of men are dying, and the Master calls for you;
> Take the task He gives you gladly; let His work your pleasure be;
> Answer quickly when He calls you, "Here am I, send me, send me."
> (Daniel March)

Day 65

For the love of money is a root of all kinds of evil. Some people, eager for money, have wandered from the faith and pierced themselves with many griefs. But you, man of God, flee from all this, and pursue righteousness, godliness, faith, love, endurance and gentleness. (1 Timothy 6:10-11)

Daily reading: Joshua 3

There is armour for the Christian so they can fight when it's appropriate. Other times, they're to flee (1 Tim.6:11; 2 Tim.2:22). Judas (Jn 12:6) and Ananias & Sapphira (Acts 5) are evidence of ruin caused by the love of money. Billy Sunday was right when he said, "The fellow that has no money is poor. The fellow that has nothing but money is poorer still." Christian, make sure there's safe distance between you and the love of money. But that's not all. *Flee* and *follow* – pursue righteousness, godliness, faith, love, endurance and gentleness.

Day 66

**The midwife took a scarlet thread and bound it on his hand.
(Genesis 38:28)
A scarlet string … for the one who is to be cleansed.
(Leviticus 14:4 NASB)
Bind this line of scarlet cord in the window. (Joshua 2:18)**

Daily reading: Joshua 4

In each verse it's a reference to the scarlet worm, the female of which attaches itself to a tree and dies while giving birth, staining the tree with its crimson body fluid. Colouring dye from her dried body was obtained long ago. This is a striking picture of the Lord's work on the cross (Ps.22:6). The life identified by the scarlet thread had been under threat but issued in birth. Ritual cleansing from leprosy required scarlet string. Sheltering behind the scarlet cord ensured a safe deliverance. Despite being sinners of the deepest dye, while deserving death we've been granted new birth; though stained we have been cleansed; and saved eternally through the one who "wrote his love in crimson red."

> O Lord, Thy love's unbounded, so full, so vast, so free,
> Our thoughts are all confounded, when'er we think of Thee.
> For us Thou cam'st from heaven for us to bleed and die,
> That, purchased and forgiven, we might ascend on high.
> Oh, let this love constrain us to give our hearts to Thee;
> Let nothing henceforth pain us but that which paineth Thee;

Our joy, our one endeavour through suffering, conflict, shame,
To serve Thee, gracious Saviour, and magnify Thy name.
(Author unknown)

Day 67

Joshua set up twelve stones in the middle of the Jordan at the place where the feet of the priests who carried the ark of the covenant were standing. (Joshua 4:9)

Daily reading: Joshua 5

Even though the Jordan was overflowing its banks during harvest time, this place - despite being the very furthest point from the calm of dry land - is emphasized as being the place where the priests' feet [were] 'standing firm' as they continued to uphold the ark of the testimony of the Lord which contained the Law. It's an appealing picture of the fact that we're privileged to be a priesthood upholding the Word of God and the testimony of Jesus (Rev.1:2;12:17) amid today's fast flowing cross-currents. Stay centred on Christ and you won't be swept away!

Day 68

Lord GOD! … I cannot speak. (Jeremiah 1:6)

Daily reading: Joshua 6

Have you not a word for Jesus? Will the world His praise proclaim?
Who shall speak if you are silent?   You who know and love His name.
You, whom He hath called and chosen His own witnesses to be,
Will you tell your gracious Master, 'Lord, we cannot speak for Thee'?
'Cannot!' though He suffered for you, died because He loved you so!
'Cannot!' though He has forgiven, making scarlet white as snow!
'Cannot!' though His grace abounding is your freely promised aid!
'Cannot!' though He stands beside you, though He says, 'Be not afraid!'
(Frances Ridley Havergal)

Day 69

A man with leprosy came to him and begged him on his knees, "If you are willing, you can make me clean." Jesus was filled with compassion. He reached out his hand and touched the man. "I am willing," he said. "Be clean!" Immediately the leprosy left him and he was cleansed. (Mark 1:40-42)

Whenever we read of the Lord Jesus being moved with compassion, we go on to read of how He was moved to action. Why did the Lord who simply commanded creation into existence also need to touch the leper? Wasn't it to support His words of compassion? The apostle James points out that words without action are useless; in fact, they might even be insulting. Are we slow at translating kind thoughts and words into action? Do our actions demonstrate our care?

> Gentleness and tender feeling, pity too and grace
> Softly lustred all Thy dealing with our stricken race.
> Thou with sympathy and healing mid our woes didst move,
> Every gracious deed revealing Thou, O Lord, art love.
> Payment meet for all we owe Thee, we, O Lord, have none;
> But we long still more to know Thee Who our hearts hast won.
> May we here, Thy love compelling, ever grateful prove,
> Walk and word and action telling Thou, O Lord, art love.
> (Cecil Belton)

Day 70

Who is this coming from Edom, from Bozrah, with his garments stained crimson? Who is this, robed in splendour, striding forward in the greatness of his strength? "It is I, proclaiming victory, mighty to save." (Isaiah 63:1)

Daily reading: Joshua 8

Yes, who is He? He's the *Eternal One* who covers Himself with light as with a garment (Ps.104:2). He's the *Kingly One* whose garments are fragrant like myrrh, aloes and cassia (Ps.45:8). He's the *Priestly One* whose beauties were foretold in the garments for glory and for beauty (Ex.28:2). He's the *Suffering One* whose garments were gambled away at the foot of His cross (John 19:24). And He's this *Conquering One* who will one day come to deliver the redeemed of Israel. At His feet we humbly fall – crown him, own Him Lord of all!

> Lamb of God, Thou now art seated high upon Thy Father's throne
> All Thy gracious work completed, all thy mighty victory won.
> Every knee in heaven is bending to the Lamb for sinners slain;
> Every voice and harp is swelling, "Worthy is the Lamb to reign."
> Lamb of God, Thou soon in glory wilt to this sad earth return;
> All Thy foes shall quake before Thee, all that now despise Thee, mourn.
> Then Thy saints appearing with Thee, with Thee in Thy kingdom reign;
> Thine the praise and Thine the glory, Lamb of God for sinners slain.
> (J.G. Deck)

Day 71

I know your works, love, service, faith, and your patience; and as for your works, the last are more than the first. (Revelation 2:19 NKJV)

Daily reading: Joshua 9

Someone said that a Christian should be like a wrist-watch: yes, they must have an open face, busy hands, be of pure gold, be well regulated, and be full of good works! We can be an example like this, and good works can adorn our lives. The letter to the Ephesians tells us that good works are like stepping-stones across the path of life, prepared by God for us to walk in. Could they be described as "good" if done out of formality or even a sense of dull duty? Surely not! Faith produces them and grace accomplishes them, so that increasingly our lives can glorify the Master.

Day 72

Present yourself approved to God. (2 Timothy 2:15)

Daily reading: Joshua 10:1-27

The people of a small mining community in Wales were served faithfully for over twenty years by their nurse. A doctor who knew her selfless work was not happy about the poor salary she was paid. One day, after a particularly arduous task, he voiced his opinions to her, 'Nurse, why don't you demand more pay? It's absurd that you receive so little. God knows you're worth it!' There was a moment's silence before she said to him, warmly but firmly, 'Doctor, if God knows I'm worth it, then that's all that matters.'

> Go, labour on; tis not for nought;
> Thine earthly loss is heavenly gain.
> Men heed thee, love thee, praise thee not;
> The Master praises; what are men?
> (Horatio Bonar)

Day 73

Christ suffered for you, leaving you an example, that you should follow in his steps. (1 Peter 2:21)

'Leaving you an example' is an interesting expression that's found here. The idea behind the word in the original language is of a parent or teacher writing the letters of the alphabet for a child to copy by writing them out again underneath in the space provided. Then Paul, by the Spirit, adds another picture: that just as a child walks behind its father, for example in the snow, so are we to 'follow (in) His steps.' It's good to see our children and grandchildren - or those of close friends - develop mentally and physically, but let's also be sure to look for Christ in the Word and so aim to develop spiritually. How well do you know your spiritual ABC's?

Day 74

The next day the whole Israelite community grumbled against Moses and Aaron. "You have killed the Lord's people," they said. But when the assembly gathered in opposition to Moses and Aaron and turned toward the tent of meeting, suddenly the cloud covered it and the glory of the Lord appeared. (Numbers 16:41-42)

Daily reading: Joshua 11

The glory appeared at exactly the time the grumblers gathered themselves together to oppose Moses. They would never have been gathered there in the first place if they hadn't previously lost sight of the glory of God. If we grumble it's at the very least a warning sign that we're losing sight of the glory of God. Whatever causes us to lose sight of God's glory will hinder our progress. Whenever the glory dims for us then our steps, too, will begin to falter.

Day 75

God understands the way to it and he alone knows where it dwells, for he views the ends of the earth and sees everything under the heavens. (Job 28:23-24)

Daily reading: Joshua 12

Be comforted, your God is El-roi: the God who sees. When your plight's undetected by your friends and when your need seems overlooked, He's there to see and oversee. Say it for yourself as Hagar did, "You are the God who sees me" (Gen.6:13).

Back of all that foes have plotted or that friends have wisely planned,
Human schemes or work of demons, moves a hidden, higher Hand:
True the Hand divine is hidden, moving secret and unseen
Through the acts of life's long drama, managing each shifting scene.
Nothing happens accidental, all that man ascribes to chance
Choice of God has first determined: nothing can escape His glance.
(Author unknown)

Day 76

So the sun stood still, and the moon stopped, till the nation avenged itself on its enemies ... There has never been a day like it before or since, a day when the Lord listened to a human being. (Joshua 10:13-14)

Daily reading: Joshua 13

The day when God listened to the voice of Joshua - God not only took note of the voice of a mere man, but He interrupted the regular movements of bodies within our solar system so that His people might be fully delivered. Maybe we can look back on a day in our experience when we knew what it was to avail ourselves of the power of God through prayer? Maybe as a result, souls were won, habits were broken, the presence of God seemed so real, or life-transforming decisions were taken? Yes, what a difference prayer can make, because God still listens to the voice of ordinary men and women. Will today be a memorable one to you through prayer?

Behold the throne of grace; the promise draws us near,
To seek our God and Father's face who love to answer prayer.
Beyond our utmost wants, His love and power can bless;
To praying souls He always grants more than they can express.
(J. Newton)

Day 77

And the fire upon the altar ... it shall not be put out ... it shall never go out. (Leviticus 6:12,13)

Daily reading: Joshua 14

Lit by God, this flame wasn't intentionally to be put out or accidentally allowed to go out. Its ongoing burning indicated that all the offerings still left Him unsatisfied. Then came the cross and the greatest Offering of all. The Sacrifice was consumed by a fire that only God could light and only God could

extinguish. At the ninth hour, fully satisfied, He caused the flame to be 'put out'
and to 'go out' - and, praise Him, it will never be re-lit!

The Lamb of God to slaughter led, the King of glory see,
A crown of thorns upon His head, they nail Him to the tree.
The Father gives His only Son, the King of glory dies
For us the guilty and undone, a spotless sacrifice.
Thy name is holy, O our God, before Thy throne we bow;
The holy place is our abode, we know Thy mercy now.
(R.C. Chapman)

Day 78

**Go home to your own people and tell them how much the Lord
has done for you, and how he has had mercy on you.
(Mark 5:19)
Let us go somewhere else—to the nearby villages—so I can
preach there also. (Mark 1:38)
Go into all the world and preach the gospel to all creation.
(Mark 16:15)**

Daily reading: Joshua 15:1-32

These are aspects of the servant's response to the Master's commission and
we can't afford to fail to notice the order: the home, the town, the world.
Lethargy in the home will never permit liberty in the town, and silence in the
town will never permit success in the world. The doorstep is the first boundary,
and living for Christ on the inside is the basis of leading men to Christ on the
outside.

If you cannot cross the ocean
Or the distant lands explore,
You can here, to needy sinners,
Tell the gospel at your door.
If to waiting crowds you cannot
Preach with eloquence the word,
You can give the printed message,
Gladly scatter for the Lord.
(Daniel March)

Day 79

And pray in the Spirit on all occasions with all kinds of prayers and requests. With this in mind, be alert and always keep on praying for all the Lord's people. (Ephesians 6:18)

Daily reading: Joshua 15:33-63

Times of prayer should be just that – "all prayer." It was the preacher D.L. Moody who spoke very bluntly about some prayer meetings that he'd been a part of: "We have a good deal of praying that is just exhorting, and if you did not see the man's eyes closed you would suppose that he was preaching." That's a big problem, because if we don't have "all prayer", how can we expect to have all answered? "I may as well kneel down and worship gods of stone, as offer to the living God a prayer of words alone." (John Burton)

Day 80

Whatever you do, work at it with all your heart, as working for the Lord, not for human masters, since you know that you will receive an inheritance from the Lord as a reward. It is the Lord Christ you are serving. (Colossians 3:23-24)

Daily reading: Joshua 16

The word 'heartily' is important. Without it we could approach our daily work as if we were just fulfilling orders. But we take our example from the life of the Lord. To tackle our responsibilities heartily means we have what's called 'skin in the game' - a personal interest and stake in what we're doing; it requires us to think about our tasks, and look for the best way to do them, remembering they're part of a divine plan that leads to heavenly reward.

> Work, for the night is coming, work through the sunny noon;
> Fill brightest hours with labour, rest comes sure and soon.
> Give every flying minute something to keep in store;
> Work, for the night is coming when man works no more.
> (A.L. Walker)

Day 81

Praise the Lord, all you servants of the Lord who minister by night in the house of the Lord. Lift up your hands in the sanctuary and praise the Lord. (Psalm 134:1-2)

Notice that these servants, the Levites, are described as ministering by night and blessing the LORD in song. It's easy to forget the fact that the tabernacle and temple were served by priests during the night as well as the day. As well as singing, the altar fire had to be kept burning, the lamps trimmed and supplied, and the whole sacred structure guarded from intruders. This service within God's house was continuing through the night hours when the world outside was dark and most would be asleep. In the New Testament 'the night' is a symbolic expression with a negative spiritual meaning. In a climate of surrounding spiritual darkness, service continues in God's house today.

Day 82

I say to myself, "The Lord is my portion; therefore I will wait for him." The Lord is good to those whose hope is in him, to the one who seeks him ... (Lamentations 3:24)

Daily reading: Joshua 18

Long is the way, and very steep the slope,
Strengthen me once again, O God of hope.
Far, very far, the summit does appear,
But You are near my God, but You are near.
And You will give me with my daily food,
Powers of endurance, courage, fortitude.
Your way is perfect, only let that way
Be clear before my feet from day to day.
(Amy Carmichael)

Day 83

... doing the will of God from your heart. Serve wholeheartedly, as if you were serving the Lord, not people ... (Ephesians 6:6-7)

Daily reading: Joshua 19:1-23

If you have a job, have you ever thanked God when you get up that you have something to do which must be done whether you like it or not! Why? Not simply because it pays the bills, although that's important. Being contracted to work and to do your best will create in you a spirit of temperance, self-control, diligence, strength of purpose and many other virtues.

Forth in Thy Name, O Lord, I go,
My daily labour to pursue;
Thee, only Thee, resolved to know,
In all I think or speak or do.
Thee may I set at my right hand,
Whose eyes my inmost substance see,
And labour on at Thy command,
And offer all my works to Thee.
(Charles Wesley)

Day 84

How precious is Your lovingkindness, O God! Therefore the children of men put their trust under the shadow of Your wings. They are abundantly satisfied with the fullness of Your house, and You give them drink from the river of Your pleasures. (Psalm 36:7-8)

Daily reading: Joshua 19:21-51

What a wonderful triplet drawing our thoughts to the provision of the Triune God: the Father who protects and cares for us; the Son who is over God's house; and the Holy Spirit whom the Lord promised as flowing from our innermost being like rivers of living water (Jn 7:38). Central to them is our entering into the satisfaction God finds in the 'fullness' of His house. The word speaks of 'fatty ashes' - the residue after sacrifice. When we come to remember our Lord Jesus in bread and wine we come as a priestly house to affirm that 'None but Christ can satisfy' both God and man.

The King of love my Shepherd is, Whose goodness faileth never,
I nothing lack since I am His and He is mine for ever.
Where streams of living water flow, my ransomed soul he leadeth;
And where the verdant pastures grow, with food celestial feedeth.
And so through all the length of days Thy goodness faileth never;
Good Shepherd, may I sing Thy praise within God's house for ever.
(H.W. Baker)

Day 85

When you leave me today, you will meet two men near Rachel's tomb, at Zelzah on the border of Benjamin. They will say to you, 'The donkeys you set out to look for have been found.' (1 Samuel 10:2)

What was the first message the newly anointed Saul received from God? It was the assurance that the donkeys he'd spent three whole days looking for were found. Saul must have thought to himself that he had much more important things to be doing! What a relief that the perplexing problem was solved. If God is asking you to begin a new venture, don't focus on what you see as being problems. If God is calling you to a mission for him, then by His enabling you can expect to find that anticipated **problems will be solved**. Plus, you might not be a champion donkey-locator, but God may want to use the gifts and abilities you do have to be a problem-solver for somebody else.

Day 86

My soul yearns, even faints, for the courts of the Lord; my heart and my flesh cry out for the living God. (Psalm 84:2)

Daily readings: Joshua 21:1-18

"Scientists claim they find everywhere the footprints of God. But who wants footprints? I want Him" (F.W. Boreham). Yes, evidence for God is one thing, but experiencing and enjoying God is another thing altogether! Any yearning for the living God was, and is, met by the Living Christ who was God manifest in flesh. Job cried, "Oh, that I knew where I might find Him." Paul told the intellectual Athenians with their altar to an unknown God that He is not far from any one of us. Christ was near enough to be touched, as lepers, sinners and blind people found out. "Where is He?" asked wise men. "We have found Him," declared Philip. To find Him is to find forgiveness, peace, satisfaction and treasure. Have you found Him yet?

How truly lovely are Thy tents, O Lord of hosts to me!
My longing soul faints for Thy courts, my heart cries out to Thee.
The sparrow and the swallow there find for their young a nest;
Thine altars, O my King and God provide for them a rest.
Who in Thy house abide are blessed, they will be praising still;
And blest is he who, trusting, loves the ways to Zion's hill.
Joy-springs and blessings mark their path along this vale of tears;
With strength renewed before their God in Zion each appears.
(Cecil Belton)

Day 87

The younger son gathered all together, journeyed to a far country, and there wasted his possessions with prodigal living. (Luke 15:13)

Daily reading: Joshua 21:19-45

Prodigal is an old-fashioned way of saying 'wasteful', but the Greek word carries the thought of widely scattering – a bit like our modern phrase 'throwing their money about'! Although it's a negative word, the parable contains more good news than bad. Why did the Lord provide these details to His hearers? So they could make a list of things not to do? No, it was to show the amazing extent of God's readiness to accept those who repent. And more than that, to display the joy in God's presence when we acknowledge our errors and turn to God for forgiveness. Of course, if we do that then we're at the same time turning away from the wrong things we've been doing. From prodigal to profitable - only God's grace can achieve that. From fallen to forgiven - the delight it brings to God was something that Christ died for.

When from the radiant throne on high
Thou didst my fall and ruin see,
Thou cam'st to earth for me to die
That I might share Thy throne with Thee;
Loved with an everlasting love,
My hopes, my joys are all above.
Oh, what is all that earth can give?
I'm called to share in God's own joy!
Dead to the world in Thee I live
In Thee I've bliss without alloy;
Well may I earthly joys resign,
All things are mine and I am Thine.
(Author unknown)

Day 88

When Abram heard that his relative had been taken captive, he called out the 318 trained men born in his household and went in pursuit as far as Dan. (Genesis 14:14)

Daily reading: Joshua 22

Did you ever wonder why Abram bothered with Lot? It seems from Genesis that the only thing Lot ever brought to Abram was a lot of trouble, and yet when a lot of trouble came to Lot Abram was there to rescue him. Abram could have been rid of a troublesome nephew without lifting a finger; instead, he instigated a major rescue mission and risked his life to save Lot, who in some translations is called his 'brother.' Do you ever wonder why God bothered with us? Love is the key in both cases. The Lord Jesus is not ashamed to call us His 'brothers' (Heb.2:11) and rescues from our sin which we're powerless to stand against alone.

Love eternal in Christ chose us,
Long ere time its race began.
Wealth of heavenly blessing shows us
What the love of God has done;
With Christ Jesus, by eternal union one.
On such love let us still ponder,
Love so great, so rich, so free;
Say. while lost in holy wonder,
"Why are we, Lord, loved by Thee?"
Hallelujah! Grace shall reign eternally.
(J. Kent)

Day 89

Going a little farther, he fell with his face to the ground and prayed, "My Father, if it is possible, may this cup be taken from me. Yet not as I will, but as you will." (Matthew 26:39)

Daily reading: Joshua 23

Behold your King! with His sorrow crowned,
Alone, alone in the valley is He.
The shadows of death are gathering round,
And the cross must follow Gethsemane.
Darker and darker the gloom must fall,
Filled is the cup, He must drink it all.
Oh, think of His sorrow! that we may know
His wondrous love in His wondrous woe.
(Frances Ridley Havergal)

Day 90

My dear children, for whom I am again in the pains of childbirth until Christ is formed in you … (Galatians 4:19)

Any mother will tell you the struggle of childbearing has very few equals. It's no wonder it's described as labour! What makes it worthwhile is the joy of seeing hearty new life in the newborn that was formed within them. And, sure enough, someone will say the baby shares the mother's characteristics! We might think any man might be living dangerously to use such an analogy, but the intensity of Paul's sadness that the Galatian disciples were not growing heartily called for such a dramatic comparison. The gospel of Christ they had believed, that had been the means of their spiritual new birth, was being replaced with error. It seemed to Paul that he had to start all over again. Would those who brought the gospel to us have the joy today of seeing something in us that shows our origin, Christ being formed in us?

Day 91

But when they looked up, they saw that the stone, which was very large, had been rolled away. (Mark 14:6)

Daily reading: Ruth 1

The disciples came to the tomb bewildered and downcast on that first Easter morning. They discussed who would roll away the stone from the door of the tomb so they could anoint the body of the One who'd been their source of hope and inspiration. But, when they looked UP, they saw that the stone had been rolled away already. Their Master was no longer in the tomb, for He'd risen triumphant over the power of death and Satan! If you want to be defeated: LOOK BACK. If you want to be depressed: LOOK INWARDS. If you want to be distracted: LOOK AROUND. But if you want to be delivered: LOOK UP! When we come to remember our risen Lord, we LOOK FORWARD to His return – bread and wine are only required until He comes!

> O God, 'tis joy to look above and see Christ on Thy throne;
> To search the heights and depths of love which He to us has shown.
> To look beyond the long dark night and hail the coming day,
> When He to all the saints in light His glories will display.
> (J.G. Deck)

Day 92

"Three men going up to worship God at Bethel will meet you ... One will be carrying three young goats, another three loaves of bread, and another a skin of wine. They will greet you and

offer you two loaves of bread, which you will accept from them." (1 Samuel 10:3-4)

Daily reading: Ruth 2

About to step out in faith upon some new enterprise for God we might be anxious about having things provided for us which we need. Again, we learn from the case of Saul that if God is in it then **provisions will be sent**. George Muller's orphanage was out of bread. After praying, there was a knock at the door; it was the baker, unable to sleep because he was sure the Lord wanted him to bake bread for Müller. "Children," Müller said, "we not only have bread, but fresh bread." Almost immediately they heard a second knock. It was the milkman; the milk cart had broken down outside the orphanage, and he offered the milk to the children, completing their meal. Perhaps God is sending you with 'provisions' for someone today?

Day 93

**Not so, Lord! (Acts 10:14)
Master ... at Your word I will. (Luke 5:5)**

Daily reading: Ruth 3

After completing his message at the crusade, the preacher Graham Scroggie remained behind as the tent emptied, leaving a solitary young woman. Sitting beside her, he asked if he could clarify anything he'd said. She answered that she knew the Lord's will, but just couldn't make up her mind to actually do it. Turning to our verse in Acts 10 and, paraphrasing, he wrote to words on a piece of paper, 'NO, Lord'. Pointing out the contradiction, he asked her to cross out one of the two words while he went to pray for her. Returning after quite some time, he found she'd crossed out, 'NO', and leaning back in her seat was repeating to herself, 'Jesus is Lord.' Which word will you cross out?

"Jesus" that name we love, Jesus our Lord;
"Jesus" all names above, Jesus our Lord.
Thou, Lord, our all must be,
Nothing that's good have we,
Nothing apart from Thee, Jesus our Lord.
(J.G. Deck)

Day 94

**Casting all your care upon Him, for He cares for you.
(1 Peter 5:7 NKJV)**

This includes all your distractions and all the things that confuse, perplex, divert, infuriate and bewilder. One of these is enough to ruin a day! By the word he used, Peter indicates that we should literally throw, or unload, our cares. Perhaps he was thinking of the time the disciples threw their coats on a colt for the Lord's journey to be made more comfortable (Lk.19:35) – it's the same word. Our great Burden-Bearer is willing to accept what makes us uncomfortable on life's journey. Why carry them around as we fume, grumble and complain? Remember, you brought to Him all of your sin burden at Calvary and He accepted it – 'not in part, but the whole.' Weymouth says in his translation: 'Throw the whole of your anxiety upon Him!' Are you ready to unload? He is ready to receive!

Day 95

Father, I thank You that You have heard Me.
(John 11:41)
I thank You, Father ... because You have ... revealed them to
babes. (Matthew 11:25)

Daily reading: Proverbs 1

We should be very wary of relying on 'positive affirmations' which focus on 'I' and are designed to convince us of our self-worth, kid us that we're self-sufficient and create in us a false sense of self-esteem to get us through tough times in life. It's far better to imitate the confident, affirmative thanksgivings of the prayers of Jesus which emphasise 'You' and not 'I.' When we need strength may we be able to pray: 'Father, I know You have this in hand, because everything is under Your control. You know what I need most of all right now, and so I claim the promise of Your supply according to Your glorious riches.' We affirm with the Psalmist that God is 'a very present help in trouble' (46:1) and bless and thank Him for 'all His benefits' (Ps.103:2).

Our times are in Thy hand, O God, we wish them there;
Our lives, our souls, our all, we leave entirely to Thy care.
Our times are in Thy hand, whatever they may be;
Pleasing or painful, dark or bright, as best may seem to Thee.

Our times are in Thy hand, Jesus the Advocate,
Nor can that hand be stretched in vain for us to supplicate.
Our times are in Thy hand; we'd always trust in Thee,
Till we, in yonder heavenly land, Thyself in glory see.
(W.F. Lloyd)

Day 96

My heart is overflowing with a good theme; I recite my composition concerning the King; My tongue is the pen of a ready writer. (Psalm 45:1 NKJV)

Daily reading: Proverbs 2

And so He gave Himself. This is the wondrous story:
The Lord for me, a slave, gave up His heavenly glory.
O Substitute divine! Thy love all loves excelling,
That gave Thy life for mine, far, far exceeds my telling.
Oh, Thy soul-consuming love my soul devour,
And from my heart self-love remove by that same power;
Its burning force my being fill with heavenly fire
That melts my pride, my stubborn will, my own desire.
(Author unknown)

Day 97

After Job had prayed for his friends, the Lord restored his fortunes and gave him twice as much as he had before. (Job 42:10)

Daily reading: Proverbs 3

Do we pray for our friends? Job did! His friends hadn't always been loyal to him, and on one occasion he even called them 'miserable comforters' (Job 16:2). But God blessed Job because of his prayers for his friends. The prophet Samuel said to King Saul, 'Far be it from me that I should sin against the LORD in ceasing to pray for you' (1 Sam.12:23). Have you stopped praying for your friends, both saved and unsaved? Watch out - you could be sinning against the Lord!

I would like you to know that you oft are remembered,
When at the dear Place interceding I bend;
Not all that you need am I able to mention,
But doesn't God know all the need of my friend?
(J. Danson Smith)

Day 98

One spoon of ... gold, full of incense. (Numbers 7:14)
His handful of the flour ... oil ... with ... frankincense ...
(Leviticus 2:2)
A certain poor widow ... threw in two mites ... (Mark 12:42)

Daily reading: Proverbs 4

Ours is a God of small things. When we remember the Lord as he commanded, we take into our hands a loaf and a cup: small things, yet so great in meaning. Among all the things of great value that the princes brought to the tabernacle dedication was the golden spoon with frankincense. At the tabernacle altar there was provision for the offerer's handful of flour, oil, and frankincense. God also delighted in the widow's two mites. Think, too, about the precious manna, that small, white, round thing! What about His incarnation? A Babe wrapped in strips of cloth lying in a manger!

Day 99

After that you will go to Gibeah of God ... you will meet a procession of prophets coming down from the high place ... and they will be prophesying. The Spirit of the Lord will come powerfully upon you, and you will prophesy with them.
(1 Samuel 10:5-6)

Daily reading: Proverbs 5

After meeting three men 'going up', Saul was to meet a group 'coming down.' It must have been quite an experience to see and hear them prophesying, and much more so to find himself participating! Like Gideon, Moses and others, we might feel our inadequacy. In fact, it would be wrong not to feel like that if the work to which we're called is God's work. Yet again, however, we can be assured from Saul's experience that in our case too, if God is calling us, then **power will be supplied** - and we'll find ourselves doing things that we thought were far beyond us.

> O Christ, Thou Heavenly Lamb, joy of the Father's heart,
> Now let Thy love my soul inflame, fresh power to me impart.
> Power to feel Thy love, and all its depth to know;
> Power to fix the heart above and die to all below.
> Power to watch and pray, "Lord Jesus, quickly come";
> Power to hail the happy day, destined to bear me home.
> (C.R. Hurditch)

Day 100

Since, then, you have been raised with Christ, set your hearts on things above, where Christ is, seated at the right hand of God. Set your minds on things above, not on earthly things. (Colossians 3:1-2)

Daily reading: Proverbs 6

Two golfers came to the tee. They could see the flag marking where the hole was on the top of a hill, but when they looked down they saw an intimidating pond of water below it. One complained to his partner, 'I know I'm going to hit this ball in the water.' His partner, trying to encourage him, told him he needed a more positive attitude. To which he replied, 'I have no problem with attitude - I'm positive I'll hit it in there!' Sports psychologists tell us that setting our mind on the wrong things will very often produce bad results. Golfers can joke that they should have taken their second shot first, but the writer was wise and serious when he encouraged us to seek the things that are above – why? Because that's WHERE CHRIST IS!

Day 101

Give me this water. (John 4:15)
Give me this portion. (Luke 15:12)
Give me a true token. (Joshua 2:12)

Daily reading: Proverbs 7

Urgency seemed to precede each of the requests in our texts. Sychar's sinful woman was beginning to realise Christ was her answer. "Give me this water." She received it - and she was **refreshed** as her inner thirst was quenched for eternity, and more. The prodigal's "Give me" proved disastrous. He squandered his inheritance and returned broken, humbled, seeking forgiveness. He received it and more - he was **restored**. Rahab, a Gentile sinner, sought a token. She received it and a scarlet cord **rescued** her from death, and more - she became part of Israel's royal line. What grace in each case! What are you urgently asking the Lord to give you?

> Give me a faithful heart, likeness to Thee,
> That each departing day henceforth may see,
> Some work of love begun, some deed of kindness done,
> Some wanderer sought and won, something for Thee.
> (S.D. Phelps)

Day 102

Those who work their land will have abundant food, but those who chase fantasies have no sense. (Proverbs 12:11)

Daily reading: Proverbs 8

We live in the world of the short-cut and the quick fix. Everywhere we look we see 'learn a language in a month', 'fast diets', 'instant loans' and 'get rich quick' schemes. It's easy to be sucked in by the lure of the short-cut. Not only is it unwise to waste time and money on these claims, which so often turn out to be a let-down in the end, but when it comes to Christian living there are no short-cuts to godliness. That's why Paul urged Timothy, "train [Greek: *gymnázō*] yourself to be godly" (1 Tim.4:7). Shallow experiences can often appear to bring us closer to God, but they're no substitute for regular and intense times spent alone with the Lord in the gym of prayer, to which you have a lifetime membership!

Oh, the pure delight of a single hour
That before Thy throne I spend,
When I kneel in prayer, and with Thee, my God,
I commune as friend with friend!
Draw me nearer, blessed Lord,
To the cross where Christ has died;
Draw me nearer, blessed Lord, to His precious, wounded side.
(Fanny Crosby)

Day 103

Carry each other's burdens, and in this way you will fulfill the law of Christ. (Galatians 6:2)

Daily reading: Proverbs 9

Now the two kinds of people on earth I mean
Are the people who lift and the people who lean.
Wherever you go, you will find the earth's masses
Are always divided in just these two classes.
And, oddly enough, you will find, too, I ween
There is only one lifter to twenty who lean.
In which class are you? Are you easing the load
Of overtaxed lifters who toil down the road?
Or are you a leaner and let others bear
Your portion of labour, and problems, and care?
(Ella Wheeler Wilcox)

Day 104

I, Tertius, who wrote down this letter, greet you in the Lord. (Romans 16:22)

Daily reading: Proverbs 10

The Bible is full of workers behind the scenes that we can only glimpse. The words of Paul in his letter to the Romans were inspired by the Holy Spirit but inscribed by Tertius – and at over 9,000 words in the English language this wasn't a small job! How valuable his painstaking work was, and how important it should be done well. He wasn't simply a hired hand either – his name could indicate his servile status, but the over-riding relationship with the author and the readers was that they were together "in the Lord." How important, too, that the letter should be safely carried to its recipients – and some wonder if Phoebe was entrusted with that task. If so, what a wonderful team effort from those in the Lord working for others in the Lord. Are you part of a team that's spreading the word of God?

Day 105

Ascribe to the Lord the glory due his name; bring an offering and come before him. Worship the Lord in the splendor of his holiness. (1 Chronicles 16:29)

Daily reading: Proverbs 11

There's no clearer instruction to those who worship God! Whether our worship's silent or spoken, we've a duty to bring an offering when we come before Him. That involves preparation because our offering will be poor if it hasn't come from a prepared heart, full of what the Lord's given us of Himself. He's worthy to receive the glory that's due to His Name, and it's our high privilege to worship the Lord in the splendour of holiness.

> O worship the Lord in the beauty of holiness,
> Bow down before Him, His glory proclaim;
> With gold of obedience and incense of lowliness,
> Kneel and adore Him: the Lord is His name.
> (J.S.B. Monsell)

Day 106

Very early in the morning, the chief priests, with the elders, the teachers of the law and the whole Sanhedrin, made their plans.

So they bound Jesus, led him away and handed him over to Pilate. (Mark 15:1)

Daily reading: Proverbs 12

This was the most important decision that this group of people would ever have to make, but it took them less time than it takes most people to decide where to go on holiday. The result - they handed the Son of God to Pilate to be crucified. Many of those present had already made up their minds during the previous three years as the crowds disowned them and followed Jesus. The elders' own pride stopped them judging correctly. Have you reached a decision about Jesus? Is He your Saviour and your Lord? Don't let pride stop you from examining the facts in the Bible, nor rush to a hasty conclusion, before making an informed decision about Jesus Christ.

Day 107

Hate evil, love good. (Amos 5:15)

Daily reading: Proverbs 13

A lot of wisdom is contained in just four words, but that doesn't mean it's easy to put them into practice. We must first recognize one from the other, as appearances can be deceiving. More wise words come from a successful gardener: 'You must not only love the flowers, but also hate the weeds'! Again, you need to know the difference between the two, for many a gardener has carefully cultivated a plant only to find out later what it truly was! Spiritually alert believers won't mistake the increasing evil which is a characteristic of the present age - 'In the last days perilous times will come ...' (2 Tim.3:1). We mustn't only just identify Satan's subtle, evil influence in many modern practices, but also weed it out so there's no place for it in our lives. At the same time, let's be encouraged to love what's of God and show by how we live where our love lies. Today, perhaps think about why there's a real danger in doing one, but not the other.

Day 108

He was in the world ... though ... the world did not recognize him. Yet to all who did receive him, to those who believed in his name, he gave the right to become children of God.
(John 1:10-12)

In Luke 4:14,37;5:15, three different words are used in the Greek to describe how the news about the Lord Jesus spread through the countryside. The first word means 'a rumour'; the second 'a stirring' and the third 'an understanding'. That's progressive. Millions have heard of Christ but to many the news is merely a rumour - little more than academic knowledge. Others are stirred into acknowledging that there are issues that are least worth exploring. Still others have reached the point of comprehending, at least in some small way, His person and work and so have received Him as their Saviour. If, by God's grace, we've reached that point, let's make every effort to reveal Him to a world that's dreadfully ignorant.

Day 109

He ordered those who could swim to jump overboard first and get to land. The rest were to get there on planks or on other pieces of the ship. In this way everyone reached land safely. (Acts 27:43-44)

Daily reading: Proverbs 15

Two hundred and seventy-six people on board this ship, including Paul, made it safely to dry land (as God promised) but not everybody did so in the same way. For some it was through swimming, others floated ashore on wooden boards, while others made use of what they could from the ill-fated ship. Difficulties can't all be dealt with in the same way. Sometimes, we're able to use our strength and swim. Other times, we feel we have to go with circumstances that we're unable to alter. Then there are the times when we're thankful of any help that's offered to us. Whatever the problem, keep going, believing that our God and Father will bring us to the safety of 'dry land.'

He sitteth o'er the waterfloods and He is strong to save;
He sitteth o'er the waterfloods, and guides each drifting wave.
Though loud around the vessel's prow the waves may toss and break;
Yet, at His word, they sink to rest, as on a tranquil lake.
He sitteth o'er the waterfloods, then doubt and fear no more;
For He who passed through all the storms
Has reached the heavenly shore.
And every tempest-driven bark with Jesus for its guide,
Will soon be moored in harbour calm in glory to abide.
(Richard Whately)

Day 110

**… there is but one God, the Father, from whom all things came and for whom we live; and there is but one Lord, Jesus Christ, through whom all things came and through whom we live.
(1 Corinthians 8:6)**

Daily reading: Proverbs 16

"… and through whom we live." What an honour to find ourselves at the end of a verse which shows the great unchanging and unique harmony of Father and Son demonstrated by their united work in creation and in their unwavering purpose for the redeemed. But do we walk harmoniously with them and live for them?

The myriad worlds unceasingly revolve at Thy command,
And none desires to wander from the leading of Thy hand,
Obedient servants are they all, they cost no thought from Thee,
But gaze upon the central sun and glide unswervingly.
But I, an atom of one world, a speck of common dust,
Cost Thee more though than all the rest, yet fail in every trust.
(Author unknown)

Day 111

No one can serve two masters, for either he will hate the one and love the other, or he will be devoted to the one and despise the other. (Matthew 6:24)

Daily reading: Proverbs 17

In Napoleon's expedition to Russia, a peasant was captured, forced into Napoleon's service and branded with the letter 'N.' When he understood what it meant, he chopped off his arm that had been branded, rather than serve his country's enemy, Napoleon. Do you know whom you are serving? Are you so committed to the Lord Jesus Christ that you would rather suffer loss than be found in the service of the enemy? Or are you attempting the impossible - to serve both?

Have you counted the cost, you warriors of the cross?
Are you fixed in your heart for the Master's sake? To suffer all earthly loss?
Can you bear the scoff of the worldly wise, as you pass by pleasure's bower,
To watch with the Lord on the mountain top through the dreary midnight hour?
(Author unknown)

Day 112

When the altar was anointed, the leaders brought their offerings for its dedication and presented them before the altar. For the Lord had said to Moses, "Each day one leader is to bring his offering for the dedication of the altar." The one who brought his offering on the first day was Nahshon son of Amminadab of the tribe of Judah. (Numbers 7:10-12)

Daily reading: 1 Timothy 1

Though there are several references in Scripture to Nahshon, this man is particularly noted in the Word of God for what may have been the highest moment in his life when he 'brought his offering on the first day.' On the first day of the week, we take our prepared offering of thanksgiving and praise (Ps.100:4). It is both a responsibility (Ex.23:15) and a privilege (John 4:23) for us to worship by the Spirit (Phil.3:3). Let's also ensure that it's recorded of us that we brought our offering on the first day.

Baskets full of firstfruits, sacrifice of praise -
Songs of our Redeemer joyfully we raise.
Lord, we come before Thee through the living way,
Worshipping with gladness on this holy day.
(J.B. Belton)

Day 113

... Gideon was threshing wheat in a winepress to keep it from the Midianites. (Judges 6:11)

Daily reading: 1 Timothy 2

It seems Gideon was someone endowed with resilience. He wasn't going to give up – even if it meant furtively threshing the wheat in a winepress! What a resourceful solution, tucked away from the prying eyes of the Midianites. But the Lord's working through Gideon, wouldn't be dependent on his natural qualities and ingenious methods, but would be effective through the known strength of the Lord's commissioning and presence: 'Am I not sending you?' (v.14) and 'I will be with you' (v.16). The progress of the Gospel today will likely demand both resilience and resourcefulness, but let's never forget that the key ingredients for success haven't changed (Matt.28:18-20).

I will never, never leave thee, I will never thee forsake,
I will guard and save and keep thee for My name and mercy's sake;
Fear no evil, only all my counsel take.
When thy soul is dark and clouded, filled with doubt and grief and care,
Through the mist by which tis shrouded,
I will make a light appear, and the banner of my love I will uprear.
(Author unknown)

Day 114

… by the power that enables him to bring everything under his control, will transform our lowly bodies so that they will be like his glorious body. (Philippians 3:21)

Daily reading: 1 Timothy 3

Michelangelo once asked a stone cutter to work for him; by painstaking direction, the unskilled cutter was told by the master-sculptor exactly how to cut and polish the marble, and eventually a beautiful sculpture emerged. 'I never realised I had such a gift,' said the cutter with a stunning lack of humility and self-awareness! Christians are waiting for their lowly bodies to be refashioned to conform to Christ's own glorious body. Just think for a moment of what that involves. Until He comes we should let our divine Master work with our lives to produce the results He desires, and happily ascribe every evidence of giftedness and every expression of grace to His careful direction.

What we in glory soon shall be, it doth not yet appear,
But when our blessed Lord we see, we shall His image bear.
With such a blessed hope in view, we would more holy be,
More like our risen glorious Lord whose face we soon shall see.
Behold what manner of love the Father hath bestowed upon us,
That we should be called the sons of God!
(Attributed to Robert Boswell)

Day 115

He gives to the beast its food and to the young ravens that cry. (Psalm 147:9)

Daily reading: 1 Timothy 4

There's nothing melodious about the cry of a raven, just a persistent, harsh 'cronk.' Yet God hears their cry and provides them with food. There was probably nothing very musical about Bartimaeus' cry either. He began to cry out and say, "Jesus, Son of David, have mercy on me!" And many told him off, telling him to be silent. But he cried out even louder, "Son of David, have mercy on me!" (Mk.10:47-48). The word used means 'cronk like a raven.' The more he was told to be silent, the louder he got. He was determined to be heard, and he was. Don't be discouraged because you think you can't pray. The God who hears and responds to a 'cronk' will surely hear you, especially if you're properly persistent.

Day 116

… a man from Bethlehem in Judah, together with his wife and two sons, went to live for a while in the country of Moab. (Ruth 1:1)

Daily reading: 1 Timothy 5

Elimelech's may have intended to seek temporary relief from famine, but decisions made in minutes can have long-lasting effects and short journeys can have far-reaching consequences. Elimelech and his family remained there and Naomi, the sole survivor, didn't return for ten years. An empty, wasted decade! Experiencing famine conditions? Take note! There's not even temporary relief in temporal things (2 Cor.4:18).

> Thou art the bread of life, O Lord to me;
> Thy holy word the truth that saveth me.
> Give me to eat and live with Thee above;
> Teach me to love Thy truth, for Thou art love.
> (Mary A. Lathbury)

Day 117

Then Joshua returned, and all Israel with him, to the camp at Gilgal. (Joshua 10:43)

Daily reading: 1 Timothy 6

Israel had been involved in a number of battles and had returned safely to their camp at Gilgal. Gilgal was a place of conscious weakness and of fellowship with God. It is when we realise our nothingness that we feel His strength. It is when we enjoy communion with our God that we receive His deliverance.

There is deliverance with Thee! I do believe it, even here - shut in, where darkness covers me, and not a human hope is near. The changeless Word of God is mine: some time again the light must shine. There is deliverance with

Thee! Against despair and fear and doubt, I do believe that I shall see - that yet Thy hand will lead me out. The place of victory is mine, I dare to trust the Word divine. (E.H. Divall)

Day 118

Enoch walked faithfully with God; then he was no more, because God took him away. (Genesis 5:24)

Daily reading: 2 Timothy 1

Enoch walked with God, not ahead of, nor lagging behind, but in step with God; moving in the same direction and in agreement with Him. Seven generations from Seth, Enoch could well have been a contemporary of Lamech. He lived at a time when men were 'successful' in spite of rebellion against God: a time of culture, of music, of technical and mechanical advancement: a godless generation when man's vengeance, self-reliance and self-satisfaction were rife. It all sounds depressingly familiar, doesn't it? We know virtually nothing about Enoch, yet he appears in the gallery of faith of Hebrews 11: "before he was taken, he was commended as one who pleased God." What a fitting epitaph "One who pleased God" would have been on his headstone if he'd needed one! Are you walking like Enoch amidst a godless generation and being found pleasing to God?

Day 119

Put some of the best products of the land in your bags and take them down to the man as a gift—a little balm and a little honey, some spices and myrrh, some pistachio nuts and almonds. (Genesis 43:11)

Daily reading: 2 Timothy 2

Jacob was a good shepherd who'd been prospered by His God. When he offered his brother, Esau, a gift, he spared nothing, but gave him a great array of breeding stock. In contrast, when he sent the present to the man on Egypt's throne it was just a little of his best, a little balm, a little honey. Had he realized the man's identity he would definitely have sent his richest treasure in abundance. Perhaps he looked back with regret later at his stinginess. How well we know the Man on the throne will likely determine the extent and value of the gifts we offer.

Bring to him life's brightest hours
He will make them still more bright;
Give to him your noblest powers,
He will hallow all your might;
Come to Him with eager quest,
You shall hear His high bequest.
(C.E. Mudie)

Day 120

...the faithful and wise manager, whom the master puts in charge of his servants to give them their food allowance at the proper time... (Luke 12:42)

Daily reading: 2 Timothy 3

It was a little after midday and the hungry travellers walked towards the village restaurant. On the door was a surprising notice: 'Closed for lunch.' This true account might seem amusing, yet it contains a vital message and illustrates something of today's text. We may be fully equipped to feed people with Scripture truth, we may even be in a position where we are the ones others would logically come to for Bible teaching, but their hunger may go unsatisfied if we are too focused on looking after ourselves. The Spirit provides spiritual food that's just right to meet the different needs each of us has. What sign will we display to hungry travellers?

Day 121

Therefore keep watch, because you do not know on what day your Lord will come. (Matthew 24:42)

Daily reading: 2 Timothy 4

After failing many times to reach his men whom he'd left on Elephant Island, the Arctic explorer Ernest Shackleton finally battled his way through the encroaching winter ice to pick them all up without a moment's delay. "Were you all ready?" he asked them later, as he marvelled at the speed of the manoeuvre. "Whenever the sea was clear," they replied, "our second-in-command instructed, 'Roll up your bags; the boss may come today.'" There's no need to pack, but are you ready?

Midst the darkness, storm and sorrow, one bright gleam I see –
Well I know the blessed morrow, Christ will come for me.
Midst the light and peace and glory of the Father's home,
Christ for me is watching, waiting, waiting till I come.
Oh, the blessed joy of meeting, all the desert past!
Oh, the wondrous words of greeting He shall speak at last!
He and I together entering those bright courts above;
He and I together sharing all the Father's love!
(Mrs. Bevan)

Day 122

**Abraham obeyed My voice and kept My charge, My commandments, My statutes, and My laws.
(Genesis 26:5)**

Daily reading: Philemon 1

If you want to make sure no one spoils your garden, you could try planting a prickly hedge all around it. That's exactly the sense of the Hebrew word we translate 'take heed', or as in today's verse: 'kept.' Abraham was a man who walked before God and who lived his life in the full view of God, just as God had told him. He treated the things God spoke to him as precious and worthy of protection. He kept them. His obedience was fervent, not forced or formal. Because of this he became God's friend. On exactly the same basis, we can become friends of Christ through loving obedience, keeping His commands, and taking care not to dilute them among other duties.

Day 123

**These searched for their family records, but they could not find them and so were excluded from the priesthood as unclean.
(Ezra 32:62)**

Daily reading: Titus 1

This is a very sad story of illegitimacy. Those mentioned in today's verse were not allowed to serve as priests when they thought they were eligible – they didn't have a record that proved it. God has been gracious beyond measure in our case. He's given us the 'right to become children of God' (Jn 1:12) and called us to serve as a priesthood too. Once we were illegitimate and unclean, not worthy of even the least service for Him. Through Christ we have been born again into His family and cleansed. No-one can take this away from us, nor can we carelessly lose the evidence of our birth – there's a record in the Lamb's Book of Life that proves it.

When we walk with the Lord in the light of His word
What a glory He sheds on our way!
While we do His good will, He abides with us still,
And with all who will trust and obey.
Trust and obey, for there's no other way
To be happy in Jesus, but to trust and obey.
(J.H. Sammis)

Day 124

Yet you, Lord, are our Father. We are the clay, you are the potter; we are all the work of your hand. (Isaiah 64:8)

Daily reading: Titus 2

Is your life taking shape under the Master Potter's hands? Like a vessel rising from an unresisting lump of clay on a potter's wheel? He moulds it with one hand inside and the other outside. What a picture of God's fatherly care. He has one hand in us, the other on us, so that internally and externally we may be shaped to His glory.

Stay still in the hand of the Potter, lie low 'neath His wonderful touch;
He moulds and He shapes in mercy, the vessel He loves so much.
Surrender yourself to His working, the curve and the hollow He wills,
Nor shrink from the pain or the pressure, for the vessel He fashions He fills.
(Martha Snell Nicholson)

Day 125

Be very careful, then, how you live—not as unwise but as wise, making the most of every opportunity, because the days are evil. Therefore do not be foolish, but understand what the Lord's will is. (Ephesians 5:15-17)

Daily reading: Titus 3

We need to be constantly reminded of the right use of time. Here's an interesting thought from Horace Mann's 'Lost, Two Golden Hours':

'Lost, yesterday, somewhere between Sunrise and Sunset,
two golden hours, each set with sixty diamond minutes.
No reward is offered, for they are gone forever.'

The solemnity of these words can only be enhanced by the thought that the American author - an active opponent of slavery and a busy proponent of educational reform - himself passed away in 1859 at the age of only 63.

Day 126

Then he said to the man, "Stretch out your hand." So he stretched it out and it was completely restored, just as sound as the other. (Matthew 12:13)

Daily reading: Jeremiah 1

Have you looked at your hands lately? Do you get a feeling of appreciation? When did you last thank God for the gift of your hands? They are a miracle, yet we take them for granted. Pause and consider your hands, then thank God for this precious gift. Rejoice, too, that you belong to the Man with the pierced hands. How busy His hands were: feeding five thousand, touching blind eyes, and finally submitting to be nailed to a cross for our redemption. When we remember Him at the breaking of bread, let us ponder those lovely, holy hands stretched out and pierced by common nails to a wooden cross, so that we could be completely restored.

Mark the earnest Workman toiling, faithful to his task and true,
Deeming nought of labour soiling that His kingly hands would do.
Man so perfect, holy, noble, humble too.
Now upon the cross suspended, see the Saviour crucified;
Slain by man His love befriended, who His agonies deride.
Yet for sinners, 'neath the wrath of God He died.
(Cecil Belton)

Day 127

And he moved from there and dug another well, and they did not quarrel over it. So he called its name Rehoboth, saying, "For now the Lord has made room for us, and we shall be fruitful in the land." (Genesis 26:22 ESV)

Daily reading: Jeremiah 2

How vital a water supply is! Three times Isaac's servants went to work digging new wells, but the first two attempts resulted in competition for the resource. Isaac named the first well "strife" and the second "opposition." He called the third well "breadths" or "room" since it was unopposed and a clear indicator to him of the Lord's blessing. Is there a lesson here? As we go about attempting to be fruitful Christians we may meet opposition as well but let's not give up. Sustained effort will result in satisfaction of thirsty hearts. We labour for the One who has the vital supply of the water of life. We can put it within reach of those who need it.

Day 128

... do not exasperate your children; instead, bring them up in the training and instruction of the Lord. (Ephesians 6:4)

Daily reading: Jeremiah 3

A man once stated his theory on raising child to the poet Samuel Coleridge. 'I believe,' he said pompously, 'children should be given a free rein to think and act and thus learn at an early age to make their own decisions. This is the only way they will grow to their full potential.' Coleridge made no comment, but simply led the man to his garden. 'Come see my flower garden,' he said. The opinionated visitor took one look at the overgrown garden and remarked, 'Why, that is nothing but a yard full of weeds.' The wise poet declared, 'It used to be filled with roses, but this year I thought I'd let the garden grow as it willed without tending to it. This is the result.' Children, like gardens, will not automatically flourish. They need daily attention and care.

Day 129

I press on toward the goal to win the prize for which God has called me heavenward in Christ Jesus. (Philippians 3:14)

Daily reading: Jeremiah 4

Forget yesterday with its triumph and failures - it's today that counts. Today will bring fresh opportunities, new aspirations and more challenges. The Lord knows your day and everything that it holds but you don't. Your responsibility is to go forward with His help and enabling to accomplish the tasks of today. Yesterday is past, tomorrow is yet to be, but today you must, 'Press on'. The Greek word used means to aggressively chase, like a hunter pursuing a catch – it's the same word the Lord used on the Damascus road to describe Paul's persecuting pursuit. Will you 'persecute' the prize today?

> Press on, never doubting; thy Captain is near,
> With grace to supply and with comfort to cheer.
> His love, like a stream in the desert, will flow,

Then stand, like the brave, with thy face to the foe.
The cause of thy Master with vigour defend,
Be watchful, be zealous, and fight to the end;
Wherever He leads thee, go, valiantly go,
And stand, like the brave, with thy face to the foe.
(Author unknown)

Day 130

As for the bronze altar that stood before the Lord, he brought it from the front of the temple—from between the new altar and the temple of the Lord—and put it on the north side of the new altar. (2 Kings 16:14)

Daily reading: Jeremiah 5

You can be sure that when God decided on one altar in a specific place He did it for a reason. The tabernacle and temple patterns He provided for Israel were unalterable because they shadowed heavenly things. That's why it was a very serious error of Ahaz to move things around, and an even more serious one to introduce an additional altar for which there was no heavenly counterpart. Yet the same thing has evidently occurred in regard to God's design for worship by a collective people under the New Covenant. From the one original Bible pattern there have been many unauthorized deviations. We're exposed to error ourselves if we don't search the Scriptures to establish God's expectations today.

Day 131

… darkness came over all the land …Jesus cried out in a loud voice, "Eli, Eli, lema sabachthani?" (which means "My God, my God, why have you forsaken me?"). (Matthew 27:45-46)

Daily reading: Jeremiah 6

And none that saw could understand
Why darkness covered all the land,
Nor those that heard that cry, 'I thirst'
Knew why the Holy One was cursed,
Nor understand those words so true,
'Father, forgive, they know not what they do'
For God above and none beside,
Knew what was done when Jesus died!
(William Walsham How)

Day 132

Then Thomas (also known as Didymus) said to the rest of the disciples, "Let us also go, that we may die with him." (John 11:6)

Daily reading: Jeremiah 7

The work of the Lord often suffers through a lack of commitment on our part. It's said that John F. Kennedy learned something about commitment from Frank O'Connor, an Irish writer, who told of his boyhood days when he and his friends would wander through the countryside. When they came to an orchard with a wall too high to climb over, they would toss their hats over the wall so that they would have no choice but to find out a way to get over! Have you tossed your hat over any walls lately?

Fight the good fight with all Thy might;
Christ is thy strength and Christ thy right.
Lay hold on life, and it shall be,
Thy joy and crown eternally.
Run the straight race through God's good grace;
Lift up thine eyes, and seek His face.
Life with its path before Thee lies,
Christ is the way and Christ the prize.
(J.S.B. Monsell)

Day 133

Zebulun will live by the seashore and become a haven for ships; his border will extend toward Sidon. (Genesis 49:13)

Daily reading: Jeremiah 8

The Zebulunites had never managed to drive out the inhabitants of the land (Judg.1:30) and over time the land of Zebulun was treated with contempt. Galilee was rightfully part of Israel but was scorned as being 'of the nations.' Yet it was to the shores of Galilee that the feet of the Lord Jesus came, and it was there He shone as a great Light to those that were in darkness. He came to seek and to save Jew and Gentile alike, choosing to dwell among the outcasts. Can anything good come from there?' (Jn 1:46), Nathanael asked about Nazareth. But he soon learned of the beauties of Jesus the Nazarene. The land of Zebulun, the haven of ships, had been graced by the Haven of souls.

Day 134

Now may the God of peace … equip you with everything good for doing his will, and may he work in us what is pleasing to him, through Jesus Christ, to whom be glory for ever and ever. Amen. (Hebrews 13:20,21)

Daily reading: Jeremiah 9

Do you ever get frustrated because of what you feel unable to do? You can conquer that frustration by accepting the inability. First of all, let the God of peace give you His peace about it, then ask that the purpose of God will give you His purpose in it. You may not always be able to do His work, but you're always able to do His will.

> The strong man's strength to toil for Christ,
> The fervent preacher's skill,
> I sometimes wish – but better far
> To be just what God will.
> (John Oxenham)

Day 135

Lord, our Lord, how majestic is your name in all the earth. You have set your glory in the heavens. (Psalm 8:1)

Daily reading: Jeremiah 10

The famous scientist Sir Isaac Newton had a perfectly scaled-down replica of the then known solar system built for his studies. A large golden ball represented the sun and the known planets revolved around it through a series of cogs, belts and rods. It was an incredible machine. One day an agnostic friend stopped by for a visit. The man marvelled at the machinery and asked, 'Who made this exquisite thing?' Without looking up, Newton replied, 'Nobody.' 'Nobody?' his friend asked incredulously. 'That's right,' Newton said, 'all of these balls and cogs and belts and gears just happened to come together, and wonder of wonders, by chance they began revolving in their set orbits with perfect timing.' The message was clear.

> The spacious firmament on high, with all the blue ethereal sky,
> And spangled heavens, a shining frame, Their great Original proclaim.
> Th'unwearied sun from day to day does his Creator's power display,
> And publishes to every land the work of an almighty hand.

What though in solemn silence all move round the dark terrestrial ball?
What though no real voice or sound amidst their radiant orbs be found?
In reason's ear they all rejoice and utter forth a glorious voice;
For ever singing as they shine, "The hand that made us is divine."
(Joseph Addison)

Day 136

And by chance there came down a certain priest that way: and when he saw him, he passed by on the other side. And likewise a Levite. (Luke 10:31,32)

Daily reading: Jeremiah 11

In the story of the 'Good Samaritan', have you ever paid attention to two small words? We're told it was 'by chance' that the priest came along, and likewise the Levite. But they were no help to the wounded man. Then came the Samaritan, but why doesn't scripture say he came 'by chance' and only that he 'came where he was' (Lk.10:33)? Isn't it because of Whom the Samaritan's intended to speak? The Lord didn't come to this world by chance, but He went out of His way to come to where we were. It wasn't by chance or some terrible accident that He went to the cross either. The Good Samaritan may have exceeded expectations in helping an enemy, but our Good Shepherd gave His life to save great sinners!

Day 137

As they were emptying their sacks, there in each man's sack was his pouch of silver! (Genesis 42:35)

Daily reading: Jeremiah 12

Joseph's brothers are not the only ones to be unaware of something valuable in their possession. William Randolf Hearst was a very wealthy newspaper publisher whose vast collection of art spoke to his insatiable desire for artistic treasure. On one occasion, he learned of some artwork he was determined to obtain and sent his agent abroad to search for the treasure. After months of investigating, the agent reported the treasure had been located and that it wouldn't cost Hearst a penny. He already owned it! The rediscovered relic was in Hearst's warehouse with many other treasures that had also never been unpacked. Lots of children of God seem to be blind to what's already in their possession. How much spiritual treasure lies unrealised.

Day 138

Therefore do not worry about tomorrow, for tomorrow will worry about itself. Each day has enough trouble of its own. (Matthew 6:34)

Daily reading: Jeremiah 13

I have nothing to do with tomorrow,
My Savior will make that His care.
Should He fill it with trouble and sorrow,
He'll help me to suffer and bear.
I have nothing to do with tomorrow,
Its burden then why should I share?
Its grace and its faith I can't borrow,
Then why should I borrow its care?
(D.W. Whittle)

Day 139

As long as it is day, we must do the works of him who sent me. Night is coming, when no one can work. (John 9:4)

Daily reading: Jeremiah 14

When the writer to the Hebrews lists the faithful in the eleventh chapter, he includes Israel. But only two instances are given – both walks of victory - the passing through the Red Sea and the fall of the walls of Jericho (Heb.11:29,30). Forty years of walking in vain lay between; forty long years brought about through faithlessness and characterised by more of the same. Yet God in His grace doesn't mention it here. He's only delighting in their faith. So He delights in ours, but what a tragedy if long wasted years lie between our early expression of victorious faith and later experiences!

In the glad morning of my day,
My life to give, my vows to pay,
With no reserve and no delay,
With all my heart I come.
Just as I am, young, strong and free,
To be the best that I can be
For truth and righteousness and Thee,
Lord of my life, I come.
(Marianne Farningham)

Day 140

Arise, let us go hence. (John 14:31 KJV)

Daily reading: Jeremiah 15

Hence! The disciples really had no idea at all what was involved in the word. But the Lord knew! For Him it meant the agony in the garden, the false trial, the abuse at the hands of men, and then on to Calvary where He would have to utter that awful cry, 'My God, My God, why have You forsaken me'? Let us, in our minds and hearts, follow Him by faith on that lonely way 'hence' to Calvary.

The Son of God, the Prince of Life, thrice in the garden prayed;
The sword was drawn to pierce the One on whom our sins were laid.
Go to Gethsemane, my soul, watch with the Saviour there;
Ponder his pretaste of the cup, then to the cross repair.
(R.C. Chapman)

Day 141

And they ... found ... the Babe. (Luke 2:16)
And they ... found not the Body. (Luke 24:3)

Daily reading: Jeremiah 16

This is the great triumph of the gospel captured in a few words by Luke at the start and at the close of his gospel. What a tragedy it would be if these statements were reversed: And they ... found not ... the Babe; And they ... found the Body. It would have meant missing the evidence of His life and keeping the evidence of death. But no, the glorious gospel is all about finding life, not facing death. Finding the Babe was the proof of His coming, while not finding the Body was the proof of His rising. So Luke ends as he began with a living Saviour – have you found Him?

We will remember His coming to earth, Immanuel!
There as a Babe we behold Him at birth, God in this world here to dwell.
Jesus, our Lord - laid in a manger, eternally God!
We will remember He rose from the dead, mighty to save.
Living for ever, our glorious Head conquered the power of the grave.
Jesus our Lord - praises for Him we present unto Thee.
(J.B. Belton)

Day 142

I called on the LORD in distress; the LORD answered me and set me in a broad place. (Psalm 118:5)

Daily reading: Jeremiah 17

Lying in bed, coughing and racked with pain, the author Robert Louis Stevenson – famous for writing Treasure Island - said to his wife, as he looked at the sunshine streaming through his windows, 'I refuse to let a row of medicine bottles be the circumference of my horizon.' By prayer, this was the psalmist's conquering experience as well. 'In distress' means being hemmed or narrowed in. The Hebrew word is only used twice in the Psalms; the other reference is to the hemming in of Hades, from which there is no escape – 'in distress' indeed! Yet here, from such a 'tight spot,' the Lord brought the writer out into a wide-open space, enlarging his view and so relieving his circumstances. There will be more than a few readers today for whom the medicine bottles loom all too large – may the Lord help you to see beyond them and enjoy the sunshine of His presence.

Day 143

… listen to this: Jesus of Nazareth was a man accredited by God to you by miracles, wonders and signs, which God did among you through him. (Acts 2:22)

Daily reading: Jeremiah 18

We might perhaps think of the word 'accredited' in connection with someone having the paperwork from an authoritative body to back up their credentials. Other translations use words such as attested, certified, approved or borne witness to. The same Greek word is used in Acts 25:27 when the Jews brought serious charges against Paul but they couldn't prove them (accredit them). What evidence did God supply to prove who Jesus was? By the many miracles He did, the greatest of which was raising Him from the dead: 'You killed the author of life, but God raised him from the dead. We are witnesses of this' (Acts 3:15). We can be witnesses too!

Day 144

No one could distinguish the sound of the shouts of joy from the sound of weeping. (Ezra 2:62)

Is the glass half full or half empty? In Ezra's day it was the younger folk who were jubilant in their joy, and the older ones were sobbing in their sorrow. The strange thing is that it was the same event that drew the two opposite reactions. Perhaps the older ones felt more responsibility for the tragedy of the past, which had led to the destruction of the old temple. Perhaps the younger ones were more focused on the potential for the future, even if the new temple didn't have the grandeur of Solomon's temple they'd never seen anyway. Young and old often still have very different perspectives on things but, as in Ezra's day, what remains absolutely vital is that the hearts of both ends of the age spectrum are moved to bring delight to the heart of God by serving Him in the way He wants us to.

Day 145

... the glorious riches of this mystery, which is Christ in you, the hope of glory. (Colossians 1:27)

Daily reading: Jeremiah 20

Has someone seen Christ in you today?
Christian, look to your heart, I pray;
The little things that you've done or said -
Did they accord with the way you prayed?
Have your thoughts been pure, your words been kind;
Have you sought to have the Saviour's mind?
The world with a criticizing view
Has watched - but did it see Christ in you?
(C.B. Hopkins)

The greatest and most glorious thing any of us can do is to live Christ.

Day 146

I counsel you to buy from me gold refined in the fire, so you can become rich ... (Revelation 3:18)

Daily reading: Jeremiah 21

The golden rule today says, 'He who has the gold makes the rules!' This cynical and self-centred version is very different from the original version: 'Do unto others as you would have them do unto you.' However, it's truer than those who coined it may have thought. In the final analysis, God's the possessor of the whole earth, and He makes the rules. One day, Satan's illusions are going to vanish and everyone will see who really has the power and the glory. We can be taken in by his scams that measure everything using money. Or we can seek from God priceless purity and live in a wealth that's measured by heaven's standards. Is it time for a visit to the Counsellor?

Day 147

The fire on the altar must be kept burning; it must not go out. Every morning the priest is to add firewood and arrange the burnt offering on the fire ... (Leviticus 6:12)

Daily reading: Jeremiah 22

Wood was an integral part of Israel's offerings. No wood, no fire, no sacrifice! "For lack of wood the fire goeth out" (Prov.26:20 RV). What a vast requirement this involved. Nehemiah appointed priests, Levites and people to bring the wood offering at specified times annually (Neh.6:10). Perhaps the wood offering could speak to us of our prepared hearts and minds, ignited by the Spirit's flame, as we contemplate Christ as the whole burnt offering of our worship. The wood was so important. So are our fragrant, appreciative thoughts of Him!

> Oh, fill me with Thy fulness, Lord,
> Until my very heart o'erflow,
> In kindling thought and glowing word,
> Thy love to tell, Thy praise to show
> (Frances Ridley Havergal).

Day 148

**We ... came ... to Philippi ... And on the Sabbath day we went ... and spoke to the women ... Lydia heard us. ... The Lord opened her heart to heed the things spoken by Paul.
(Acts 16:11-14)**

Daily reading: Jeremiah 23

The story of Paul and Lydia reveals the greatness of the boundless Word of God (2 Tim.2:9) - from an opened heart there flowed an opened home and an opened continent as the Word spread into Europe. No matter how apparently unimportant it might seem when the message is given to one person, we must always remember that seemingly simple though it is, the results that follow may be sublime. 'In the morning sow your seed, and in the evening do not

withhold your hand; for you do not know which will prosper, either this or that,
or whether both alike will be good' (Eccles.11:6).

Sow in the morn thy seed, at eve hold not thy hand,
To doubt and fear give thou no heed, broadcast it o'er the land.
Thou know'st not which may thrive, the late or early sown;
Grace keeps the chosen germ alive, when and wherever strewn.
And duly shall appear in verdure, beauty, strength,
The tender blade, the stalk, the ear, and the full corn at length.
Thou cast not toil in vain; cold, heat, and moist, and dry,
Shall foster and mature the grain for garners in the sky.
(J. Montgomery)

Day 149

... we wait for the blessed hope—the appearing of the glory of our great God and Savior, Jesus Christ ... (Titus 2:13)

Daily reading: Jeremiah 24

The fishing boats were returning to harbour; a group of the fishermen's wives were watching at the quayside. Soon, joyful reunions took place. But not for Angus. There was no one to meet him, so he went on his way alone. Arriving at home, his wife welcomed him warmly. 'I was waiting for you, Angus!', she said. 'Aye', he replied, 'but Willie's wife was watching for him'! Are we watching as well as waiting for the Master?

Are we watching for the Master?
For his coming draweth near;
Are we ready for the moment
When He shall for us appear?
(Isobel Hickling)

Day 150

Let the peace of God rule in your hearts. (Col.3:15)
Let the word of Christ dwell in you richly. (Col.3:16)
Let your speech always be with grace. (Col.4:6)

Daily reading: Jeremiah 25

LET! LET! LET! In other words, don't hinder peace or grace from entering our hearts and our lives. Allow them an open path into our daily Christian experience. Notice Paul's repetition of the word 'Let' in the space of a few verses of his letter to the Colossians. It means to admit, to allow, to grant permission. Sometimes three-letter words carry great power, and open doors of help to new experiences. The opposite meaning is to prevent, oppose, raise a barrier. As Christians, let's follow the positive to know joy, peace, and blessing. Let peace rule within **me**! Let God's word dwell in **me** richly! Let **my** speech be always with grace!

Let not your heart be troubled, nor let it be afraid;
Believe in God, My Father, believe what I have said,
My Father's house hath many a mansion bright and fair;
And I am going yonder a place now to prepare.
(Charles Mann Luxmoore)

Day 151

After this, the word of the Lord came to Abram in a vision: "Do not be afraid, Abram. I am your shield, your very great reward." (Genesis 15:1)

Daily reading: Jeremiah 26

Abram knew the glory of God's protection and the greatness of God's reward. Unlike Rehoboam, Abram knew that his Shield had no equivalent. Judah's king replaced three hundred shields of gold with brass replicas (1 Kin.14:26,27). To others they may have looked, measured and weighed the same, but brass isn't gold. Likewise, the Christian may shield himself with foolhardiness and it may not be detected. But foolhardiness isn't faith (Eph.6:16). Our God-given protection has no equal so, like David, we may say, "My shield is with God" (Ps.7:10 RV)."

O worship the King all-glorious above,
O gratefully sing his power and his love:
Our shield and defender, the Ancient of Days,
Pavilioned in splendor and girded with praise.
Frail children of dust, and feeble as frail,
In you do we trust, nor find you to fail.
Your mercies, how tender, how firm to the end,
Our Maker, Defender, Redeemer, and Friend!
(Robert Grant)

Day 152

For you, God, tested us; you refined us like silver ... we went through fire and water, but you brought us to a place of abundance. (Psalm 66:10-12)

Daily reading: Jeremiah 27

I know not why His hand is laid in chastening on my life,
Nor why it is my little world is filled so full of strife,
But I do know that God is love, that He my burden shares,
And though I may not understand, I know for me He cares.
I know the heights for which I long are often reached through pain.
I know that sheaves must first be threshed to yield the golden grain.
I know that, though He may remove the friends on whom I lean,
'Tis thus that I may learn to love and trust the One unseen.
And when, at last, I see His face and know as I am known,
I will not care how rough the road that led me to my home.
(Grace Troy)

Day 153

Be careful not to harbor this wicked thought: "The seventh year, the year for canceling debts, is near," so that you do not show ill will toward the needy among your fellow Israelites and give them nothing. (Deuteronomy 15:9)

Daily reading: Jeremiah 28

Can you imagine this happening in today's society? Every seven years signalled a release of debts in Israel - every creditor who'd lent anything to his neighbour wasn't to require its return anymore. In year six it might have been very tempting not to make any loans for fear it wouldn't be paid back in time. God describes such a thought as a 'wicked thought.' "You shall surely give to him" (15:10) was still the instruction from the God who has no self-interest and who "did not spare his own Son, but gave him up for us all" (Rom.8:32). Paul asks if he did that won't he "graciously give us all things"? Next time you're inclined to put limits on your generosity, check your motives. A generous giver needs neither a calendar nor a calculator, only a conviction that - one way or the other – the Lord is no man's debtor.

Day 154

And when ... they saw the young Child ... fell down and worshipped Him. (Matthew 2:11)
They drew back and fell to the ground. (John 18:6)

Daily reading: Galatians 1

Abram, Moses, Aaron, Joshua and Ruth belong to a reverent Old Testament procession of those who knew their proper place - falling on their faces before God or the Redeemer. Then, when the Son of God came to earth, so did another reverent procession. Among them, a father, a mother, a leper and disciples, each falling at His feet. In contrast, there came a crowd to Gethsemane - and they fell as well. Unable to fall forward as worshippers, they fell backward as irreverent rejecters. What a Saviour! He causes all to fall.

Who is He in yonder stall,
At whose feet the shepherds fall?
'Tis the Lord! O wondrous story!
'Tis the Lord! the King of glory!
At His feet we humbly fall,
Crown Him! Own Him Lord of all!
(Benjamin R. Hanby)

Day 155

Another king arose who did not know Joseph. (Acts 7:18)

Daily reading: Galatians 2

'I didn't know' isn't a good excuse, but it's used very often. Perhaps we've overlooked the deep grief hidden behind a friend's eyes. Perhaps, like Peter, we might have said we didn't know the Lord in circumstances when our discipleship was being tested. Even the Lord of glory was crucified because people didn't know who He was, but to know Him is to find blessing. Joseph had once been well known as the great deliverer from famine, but subsequently he was forgotten and his people were enslaved. Our Deliverer is now largely unknown, and some speak of our days as the post-Christian era. Tell them! Too soon it will be too late for anybody to protest, 'If only I'd known.'

Day 156

The Lord is my rock, my fortress and my deliverer; my God is my rock, in whom I take refuge, my shield and the horn of my salvation. He is my stronghold, my refuge and my saviour ...
(2 Samuel 22:3)

Daily reading: Galatians 3

The presence of God is like a prayer-enclosure with its surrounding fence and gate for our protection. Tragically, we can suffer the consequences if we risk living outside of it. Henry Durbanville said, 'A fence at the top of a precipice is better than a hospital at the bottom', and George Muller emphasised that, 'The morning is the gate of the day and should be well guarded by prayer'. Let's live inside the fence, inside the gate!

From every stormy wind that blows,
From every swelling tide of woes,
There is a calm, a safe retreat -
Tis found beneath the mercy seat.
(H. Stowell)

Day 157

And the people were faint. (1 Samuel 14:28 KJV)
And the people were very faint. (1 Samuel 14:31 KJV)
Men ought always to pray, and not to faint. (Luke 18:1 KJV)

Daily reading: Galatians 4

These verses indicate there are degrees of 'fainting.' Physically, faintness can indicate an issue with the heart – and it's the same spiritually. The Greek word used in Luke 18 can be translated as 'lose heart.' Even though we know this is one of the Devil's tactical weapons against us, linked with his aim to make us feel defeated and unworthy, we find it hard to overcome. Can it be done? Yes! How? By degrees of force? No. By degrees of faith? No. By prayer, and there's only one degree of it - 'ALWAYS'!

Though many foes best us round and feeble is our arm,
Our life is hid with Christ in God, beyond the reach of arm.
Weak as we are we shall not faint, or, fainting, shall not fail;
Jesus, the strength of every saint, for ever must prevail.
As surely as He overcame, and conquered death and sin,
So surely those who trust His name shall all His triumph win.
(John Newton)

Day 158

Then Pharaoh took his signet ring from his finger and put it on Joseph's finger. He dressed him in robes of fine linen and put a gold chain around his neck. (Genesis 41:42)

Daily reading: Galatians 5

Both Joseph's glorious coat of many colours and his humble servant's outfit were stolen from him. In their place were prison clothes and bands of iron. But in God's purposes, the day came for fine linen, gold and an exalted position of authority. The grace of Joseph is a beautiful picture of the Lord Jesus, who left his home and laid aside his glory to become a servant. Joseph gave his brothers the very things they took from him: clothes, a home and freedom from want. 'Do not be afraid,' he said, 'I will provide for you and your little ones.' Let us tell the Lord how much we appreciate His grace and provision for us today – robes of righteousness, a heavenly home and abundant blessings.

Day 159

This is a desert place ... he went up into a mountain apart to pray ... the ship was now in the midst of the sea. (Matthew 14:15-24 KJV)

Daily reading: Galatians 6

"Desert ... mountain ... sea" – each was an unlikely sounding place in which to learn from the Lord. In reality, He'll meet us in all today's varied circumstances, however extreme they are.

> The desert place, the mountain lone, the troubled sea,
> These are Thy schools, there I may learn of Thee.
> The broken Bread, the Prayer on high, the outstretched Hand;
> The hungry fed, the sinking saved, the ship at land;
> The baskets filled, the waves subdued, the tempest past;
> The plan, the power, the grace from first to last;
> I con my lesson o'er, and still spell out
> 'O thou of little faith, why didst thou doubt?'
> (Christina Rossetti)

Day 160

And all Israel from Dan to Beersheba knew that Samuel had been established as a prophet of the LORD. (1 Samuel 3:20 NKJV)

Daily reading: Hosea 1

What amazing exploits led up to this lofty appointment? Actually, it was a lot of keeping charge of the tabernacle (Num.1:53), attending to service (Num.18:2) and to duties (2 Chron.13:10). Yes, duties! No doubt Samuel faced many more difficult mornings after the one when, having opened the doors of the tabernacle (1 Sam.3:15), he was required to tell Eli the Lord's words, but as a true Levite, he did 'as the duty of each day required' (2 Chron.8:14). 'The duty of each day'! That's how true growth is achieved. As the poet George MacDonald said, "Life is not a blaze of sudden glory won, but an adding up of days in which God's will is done." So, how many days have you added up so far?

Fill Thou my life, O Lord my God, in every part with praise,
That my whole being may proclaim Thy being and Thy ways.
Praise in the common things of life, its goings out and in;
Praise in each duty and each deed, however small and mean.
(Horatius Bonar)

Day 161

**I am poured out like water. (Psalm 22:14)
... a woman came to him with an alabaster jar of very expensive perfume, which she poured on his head as he was reclining at the table. (Matthew 26:7)**

Daily reading: Hosea 2

As a Servant, He'd poured water into a basin to wash His disciples' feet, a sign of the depth of his servanthood. As Saviour, He was 'poured out like water' – a prophetic expression which seems to breathe the depths of His sufferings. That He 'poured out His soul unto death' (Is.53:12 NKJV) declares the depths he was prepared to go to complete the work of salvation. Paul spoke about being poured out as a drink offering (Phil.2:17) – indicating the depth of appreciation that he had for the sacrifice of Calvary. And you? And me? Can we - dare we - hold anything back? Rather, on this Lord's Day, shall we do as the woman did and pour out our treasure in worship, glorifying the God and Father of our Lord Jesus Christ?

Day 162

Then Jesus said to his disciples, "Whoever wants to be my disciple must deny themselves and take up their cross and follow me. (Matthew 16:24)

Daily reading: Hosea 3

For James, John and Simon, it was time to give everything up: boats, nets, sea and fish. They'd become vessels under new Captaincy; the message of the gospel had become their nets; towns and villages had become their fishing ground; men had become their catch instead of fish. They couldn't take up their past oars and their present cross at the same time. Nor can we.

I cannot hope to follow Thee unless
I first deny myself, take up my cross
Each day, and heed afresh Thy just command,
"Come, follow Me", though I may suffer loss.
(Timothy Dudley Smith)

Day 163

Should you then seek great things for yourself? Do not seek them. (Jeremiah 45:5)

Daily reading: Hosea 4

Though deaf and blind from around 18 months old, Helen Keller once said, "I long to accomplish some great and noble task, but it is my chief duty and joy to accomplish humble tasks as if they were great and noble … for the world is moved along, not only by the mighty shoves of its heroes, but also by the aggregate of tiny pushes of each honest worker." Do you think your honest labour goes unnoticed, and does that trouble you? If the world ignores its ordinary folk, doing ordinary things in ordinary ways, take heart – there is One who takes notice. After all, working for Him is the occupation of 'transforming commonplace affairs into the business of the King' as Edgar King put it.

I would not have the restless will that hurries to and fro,
That seeks for some great thing to do, or secret thing to know;
I would be treated as a child and guided where to go.
Wherever in the world I am, in whatso'er estate,
I have a fellowship with hearts to keep and cultivate;
And a work of lowly love to do for the Lord on whom I wait."
(A.L. Waring)

Day 164

Dorcas ... full of good works. (Acts 9:36)
Whose faith follow. (Hebrews 13:7)
Show me your faith without your works. (James 2:18)

Daily reading: Hosea 5

Our Bible teaches us that people can be full of envy, joy, indignation, comfort, and the Holy Spirit. But Dorcas was 'full of good works and charitable deeds' as a nimble seamstress! Her name means 'a gazelle'; in fact there's even such a thing as a Dorcas gazelle - a nimble, bright-eyed, gentle creature - and such she must have been, someone with a real spring in their step and a twinkle in their eye! Christians wept when she died, and God graciously restored her to life at the behest of her friends and Peter. What a testimony! What will they say about me, and you? That's a challenging question, isn't it?

Day 165

The Lord told him, "Go to the house of Judas on Straight Street and ask for a man from Tarsus named Saul, for he is praying."
(Acts 9:11)
You have made your way around this hill country long enough; now turn north. (Deuteronomy 2:3)

Daily reading: Hosea 6

It's true to say that the unbeliever goes round in circles until, like Saul, he's brought to Straight Street. Sadly, the believer can go round in circles as well, wasting precious years of potential progress in meaningless meanderings. "For a long time we made our way around the hill country." A long time? Well, it was over fourteen and a half thousand days to be more precise! No wonder the LORD said, "You have made your way around [gone round in circles] this hill country long enough." Believer, no matter how long you've been 'revolving', it's 'long enough.' Abandon revolving, ask for reviving. Don't go round, 'go forward' instead (Ex.14:15).

Day 166

One night the Lord spoke to Paul in a vision, "Do not be afraid; keep on speaking, do not be silent."
(Acts 18:9)

What shall be our word for Jesus? Master, give it day by day;
Ever as the need arises, teach Thy children what to say.
Give us holy love and patience; grant us deep humility,
That of self we may be emptied and our hearts be full of Thee;
Give us zeal and faith and fervour, make us winning, make us wise,
Single-hearted, strong and fearless, Thou hast called us, we will rise!
Let the might of Thy good Spirit go with every living word;
And by hearts prepared and opened be our message always heard!
(Frances Ridley Havergal)

Day 167

Peter took him aside and began to rebuke him. "Never, Lord!" he said. "This shall never happen to you!" (Matthew 16:22) "Master, we have toiled all night and caught nothing; nevertheless at Your word I will let down the net." (Luke 5:5)

Daily reading: Hosea 8

Our texts refer to two occasions when Peter argued with the Lord – that's never a good idea! Though he spoke with the best of intentions, he should have known never to say 'Never' to the Lord. In the boat (Lk.5), his protest was shorter and less vehement and he seems quickly to have thought better than to press his point, preferring to submit to His Lord's command. Has the Lord been asking you to do something and even by your delay you've raised objections? You'll be far happier, and He'll be glorified, if you turn your 'Never,' into 'Nevertheless.'

Have Thine own way, Lord, have Thine own way;
Thou art the Potter, I am the clay.
Mould me and make me after Thy will,
While I am waiting yielded and still.
(A.A. Pollard)

Day 168

Joseph ... with bitterness archers attacked him; they shot at him with hostility. But his bow remained steady, his strong arms stayed limber ... (Genesis 49:22-24)

Joseph's brothers are compared to archers who let fly their arrows for maximum injury. They succeeded in causing him hurt and grief. Did you notice the absence of any mention of Joseph's arrows? There is none because retaliation wasn't in Joseph's character. Remember what Peter wrote about our 'Joseph': 'When they hurled their insults at him, he did not retaliate; when he suffered, he made no threats. Instead, he entrusted himself to him who judges justly.' As we worship the God and Father of the Lord Jesus, let us remember He endured both the cross and the violence of sinners yet 'his bow remained steady, his strong arms stayed limber …'

Day 169

Nevertheless He did not leave Himself without witness. (Acts 14:17)

Daily reading: Hosea 10

They've got no mouths, eyes, ears, hands or feet, and they're known throughout the world. What are they? Idols? No: in fact, they're among God's most faithful witnesses - even though they never utter a word. They are the seasons and elements which together declare a Maker and a Maintainer. And they serve the same Lord who called other witnesses who have mouths, and eyes, and ears, and hands, and feet to testify about Him. Fellow-Christian, let your witness be audible and visible because it's an honour given to you in the great commission of the God of the 'Nevertheless.'

All heaven on high rejoices to do its Maker's will;
The stars with solemn voices resound your praises still.
So let my whole behavior, each thought, each deed I do,
Be, LORD, my strength, my Savior, a ceaseless song to you.
(Thomas R. Birks)

Day 170

I served the Lord with great humility and with tears and in the midst of severe testing by the plots of my Jewish opponents. (Acts 20:19)

Daily reading: Hosea 11

Those whose hearts are most deeply moved are most likely to move the heart of God, for they pray like the Man of Sorrows. How much we need to remember Thomas Brooks' warning: "Cold prayers always freeze before they reach heaven"! May God melt us until our prayers are distilled from thawed hearts, through tears.

We plead before our Father's face,
Close to Him at His throne of grace,
Yet nearer come when burdens, fears,
Are shared by praying – and with tears.
(Author unknown)

Day 171

He shall prepare a grain offering ... as much as he wants to give. (Ezekiel 46:7)

Daily reading: Hosea 12

The phrase 'as much as he wants to give' literally means as much as his hand can reach. Those who give begrudgingly are sometimes accused of having short arms and deep pockets! That means they can't reach very far! Thankfully, it's not so with God. He gave us His very best in Jesus. There's no limit on the praise we can give to Him, neither on time. When it comes to giving of any form, we should be a people with long arms and deep pockets.

Day 172

... one thing I do: Forgetting what is behind and straining toward what is ahead ... (Philippians 3:13)

Daily reading: Hosea 13

Have you ever tried cycling while facing backwards and sitting on the handlebars? It's not recommended unless you're prepared to fall off! This sounds totally obvious, yet sometimes we can attempt to live the same way by forever looking backwards. It's very difficult to steer in the right direction if we continually look at the wrong turns or falls of the paths we've already taken, or to enjoy the views of past scenes of victory. We're not told Paul ever became downcast as he remembered his part in Stephen's death or in persecutions of other Christians. Nor did he become preoccupied with spiritual successes. His godly service would imply he didn't because it's impossible to be effective for the future without letting go of the past. If you're having trouble with the past – its guilt or its glories - ask the Lord to help turn you around.

Day 173

As they talked and discussed these things with each other, Jesus himself came up and walked along with them.
(Luke 24:15)

Daily reading: Hosea 14

Not an angel from the glory, flying swift on joyous wing;
Not an envoy sent expressly, with a message from the King;
But Himself Whom angels worship;
But Himself, the very Word;
All divine, intensely human, sympathising, risen Lord.
Coming slowly, gently, lowly, He to Whom all power is given,
Strong to save thee, wise to guide thee,
Pledged to bring thee safe to heaven;
Coming nearer than thy nearest,
Those who would, but cannot, aid.
Proving truer than thy dearest,
Those who watched with thee and prayed.
No more doubtings, no more distance,
No more room for sinful fear:
He Himself is thine for ever, always able, always near.
(Author unknown)

Day 174

A man who was full of leprosy ... fell on his face and implored Him, saying, 'Lord, if You are willing, You can make me clean.'
(Luke 5:12)

Daily reading: Ephesians 1

You couldn't have accused this man of rambling, being vague or too general in the petition he brought to the Lord. Even outside of remotely comparable dramatic circumstances, it serves as a reminder and example of a focused request delivered with real passion and urgency. The word translated as 'implored' appears in Luke 10:2 when the Lord told his disciples to implore the Lord of the Harvest to send workers, and also in Luke 22:32 when He prayed (implored) for Peter that Satan wouldn't sift him as wheat. Both these things were matters of great importance. How much do our prayers, and the answers we're asking for, really matter to us – and, for that matter, to God?

Day 175

**Get a potter's earthen flask ... go out to ... the Potsherd Gate;
and ... break the flask. (Jeremiah 19:1,2,10)
My strength is dried up like a potsherd. (Psalm 22:15)**

Daily reading: Ephesians 2

There was drama with the pathetic end of Judas at the Potter's Field, but the Potter's flask was God's graphic demonstration through the prophet Jeremiah to the elders of Israel at Jerusalem that, because of their atrocities in the valley of Hinnom, He was going to shatter them, dashing their own future plans to pieces. Our sins meant that we deserved the same treatment, but there was One who was willing to be shattered in our place when crushed for our iniquities upon the cross. Praise the Lord today for He's made us whole!

Day 176

**Preach the Word. (2 Timothy 4:2)
... you will be my witnesses in Jerusalem, and ... to the ends of
the earth." (Acts 1:8)**

Daily reading: Ephesians 3

The preacher is a herald. It's their responsibility to proclaim a royal message, but they have to know the message before they're able to preach it or else the result will be a royal mess! There must be no doubt about the message we preach, nor may we shrink or stretch it, bend or amend it, spin or twist it, or otherwise modify it. God's Word is clear. His testimonies "stand firm" (Ps.93:5). Jesus said, "whatever I say is just what the Father has told me to say." (Jn 12:50). Can you say the same?

> Oh, teach me, Lord, that I may teach
> The precious things Thou dost impart;
> And wing my words that they may reach
> The hidden depths of many a heart.
> (Frances Ridley Havergal)

Day 177

**Open my eyes that I may see wonderful things in your law.
(Psalm 119:18)**

A famous landscape artist was once told by a skeptical lady, "I do not see in nature the colours you depict in your paintings." He replied, "Don't you wish you did, madam?" Ouch! The Christian's heart should thrill at the new and precious things revealed in God's Word. If we're finding what we read drab and lifeless, and perhaps even distant from reality, then it's our spiritual vision that's the problem! We must always pray: 'Open my eyes that I may see.' Awareness is the key. It enables us to be alert and sensitive to the Spirit's help. Let us be thankful for every precious thought as we pray:

> Oh, may the heavenly pages be our ever new delight!
> And still new beauties may we see and still increasing light.
> (Anne Steele)

Day 178

Preserved (kept, R.V.) in Jesus Christ. (Jude v.1)
Now to Him who is able to keep you from stumbling.
(Jude v.24)
Keep yourselves in the love of God. (Jude v.21)

Daily reading: Ephesians 5

Three keepings - past, present and future. All who are 'in Christ' are kept (Greek: téreó – used of the guards at the cross and the Easter tomb) safe and secure in His love. And He's able to continue to keep us (Greek: phulassó – used of the constant vigilance of the shepherds in Luke 2:8) until He presents us faultless before the presence of His glory. Until that glorious time we have a responsibility to keep (téreó) ourselves, not 'in Christ' or in salvation, for that's in His keeping, but in the love of God; in other words to abide in Christ so that nothing hinders our enjoyment of His love. 'The Lord shall preserve (keep, RV) your going out and your coming in, from this time forth, and even for evermore' (Ps.121:8).

> To Him who is able to keep us - His called ones,
> Preserved in Christ Jesus, the saints of the Father -
> To keep us from falling and faultless to set us
> Before His bright glory with fullness of joy.
> To the Lord God who keepeth midst sin and in weakness,
> Whose wisdom alone is, to God and our Saviour,
> Be majesty, glory, dominion and power,
> Both now and for ever, Amen, amen.
> (Naylor)

Day 179

I am full of matter. (Job 32:18 KJV)

Daily reading: Ephesians 6

Yes, it's tough when you're misinterpreted, and it's hard to take when you're misunderstood. Being called an 'empty man' must have added insult to injury for Job, after being told that he was 'a man full of talk.' It was like saying 'You're all mouth' to a man who was 'all heart.' Thankfully, there are no misconceptions with God. Even His Son showed that silence is the best answer when men accuse and choose not to listen.

Canst thou endure the furnace of affliction,
Still looking upward with a trusting smile?
Learn now to be for Christ in faith and patience,
And put aside the doing for a while.
(Nora Hanssen)

Day 180

See, I am sending an angel ahead of you to guard you along the way and to bring you to the place I have prepared. (Exodus 23:20)

Daily reading: Deuteronomy 1:1-18

When all the sky is clear to view, and waters calm, and trials few,
We sing with joy, "'Tis surely true, that God does lead the way".
But when sore trial starts the day, do we a fainting heart display?
Do we begin to doubt and say, "Does God now lead the way"?
We may not see our Father's hand, by Whom our way through life is planned.
Yet soon in heaven we'll understand just why He led that way.
His way is right, His way is best – why not upon His promise rest?
Should He not grant us our request, He leads the better way.
And when our tale of life is told, the silver, costly stones and gold
Will at the Judgement-seat unfold His leading of the way.
(Annie Johnson Flint)

Day 181

He said to them, "When I sent you without purse, sack, and sandals, did you lack anything?" So they said, "Nothing." (Luke 22:35)

A common sign outside North American restaurants warns potential diners "No shoes? No service!" Ironically, one establishment is called "Shoeless Joes" after the iconic baseball player. Evidently, the disciples had no shoes, but that didn't rule out service! Not only would they lack the Master's reassuring physical presence, they didn't even have the basics for a road-trip. To their credit, they obediently went anyway, and must have been astonished as they found that everything had been taken care of. The Master had sent them, and He accepted responsibility for them. Provided they walked in His way and obeyed His Word, He was bound by the promise 'no good thing does He withhold' (Ps.84:11). And so with us. 'My God shall supply all your need according to His riches in glory by Christ Jesus' (Phil.4:19).

> Oh, teach us, Lord, to wait Thy will,
> To be content with all Thou doest;
> For us Thy grace sufficient still,
> With most supplied when needing most.
> (Author unknown)

Day 182

How good it is to sing praises to our God ... (Psalm 147:1)

Daily reading: Deuteronomy 2

It's been said that swans sing energetically at the end of their lives, albeit perhaps not overly melodiously; thus the possible origin of the word 'swansong.' Singing is an integral part of the Christian's life. We're to make melody in our hearts with psalms, hymns and spiritual songs. What a repertoire we have to choose from! Singing is so much better than complaining, deriding or grumbling. Singing from the heart covers all conditions of the human voice. Sing today - whether you're a skylark or a crow - unto the Lord!

> I will sing of my Redeemer and His heavenly love to me;
> He from death to life hath brought me, Son of God with Him to be.
> (P.P. Bliss)

Day 183

**His disciples came to Him and said, "Send the crowds away."
(Matthew 14:15)
So his disciples came to him and urged him, "Send her away.
(Matthew 15:23)**

But the disciples rebuked them. (Matthew 19:13)

Daily reading: Deuteronomy 3

The Adversary never gives up, does he? Having failed in the direct temptation of the Lord, he tried the indirect approach in other desert conditions. It was sad that disciples who knew most about the Saviour's kindly provision (14:15), mercy (15:23) and intercessory touch (19:13), should tell Him to discourage others from discovering them too. It would be tragic if unbelievers ever see that barrenness is within us and not only around us!

My life shall touch a dozen lives before this day is done,
Leave countless marks of good or ill, e'er sets the evening sun.
This, the wish I always wish, the prayer I always pray;
Lord, may my life help others lives, it touches by the way.
(Strickland Gillilan)

Day 184

**While we were still sinners, Christ died for us. (Romans 5:8)
Take My yoke upon you and learn from Me. (Matthew 11:29)**

Daily reading: Deuteronomy 4:1-24

The poster on the church's noticeboard read, 'God might feed the birds, but He doesn't throw food into the nest!' Yes, God in His grace, and through the atoning death of Christ, did for us what we couldn't do for ourselves – He made us born again spiritually. As Christians we're then provided with food - God's Word – and in the early days we rely heavily on others to bring it to us. It will involve work, but there comes a point that we should 'fly the nest' and learn to find the food and feed ourselves so that we 'grow in the grace and knowledge of our Lord and Saviour Jesus Christ' (2 Pet.3:18). Don't be lazy, be a learner!

Day 185

**They have addicted themselves to the ministry of the saints.
(1 Corinthians 16:15 KJV)**

Daily reading: Deuteronomy 4:25-49

The 1611 translation's eye-catching, although perhaps a bit misleading for modern readers. The Greek word translated as 'addicted' means 'to arrange in an orderly manner' with reference to a military operation. It's proactive, not reactive, just as an addict goes out of their way to ensure their next need of drugs or alcohol will be met. Are you proactively 'addicted' to God's saints?

Some are hurting. Do you care? Some are sorrowing. Will you comfort? Some are perplexed. Can you counsel? Some are lonely. Should you visit? Some are struggling. Are you praying? Some are wandering. Are you searching? Some are heart-broken. Are you weeping? Big helpers have big hearts. We'll be addicted to the degree that we're affected.

> Christian pity moves our heart through the love of Christ;
> Others' woes pierce like a dart, when there's love to Christ.
> We will love with tender care, knowing love to Christ,
> Brethren who his image bear, for the love of Christ.
> (Author unknown)

Day 186

… the solid foundation of God stands, having this seal: "The Lord knows those who are His," and, "Let everyone who names the name of Christ depart from iniquity."
(2 Timothy 2:19 NKJV)

Daily reading: Deuteronomy 5

By the unalterable foundation of God's true word believers are eternally secure. They are His. They will never hear that final, irrevocable, "Depart from Me." However, Christians have present departures to make. We're commanded to "depart from iniquity" and elsewhere flee fornication, idolatry and youthful lusts because "this is the will of God, your sanctification" (1 Thess.4:3 NKJV). Security is a present reality, but sanctification is still a present necessity.

> More purity give me, more strength to o'ercome;
> More freedom from earth stains, more longings for home.
> More fit for the kingdom, more used would I be,
> More blessed and holy; more, Saviour, like Thee.
> (P.P. Bliss)

Day 187

Therefore the Lord himself will give you a sign: The virgin will conceive and give birth to a son, and will call him Immanuel.
(Isaiah 7:14)

Daily reading: Deuteronomy 6

> Matchless grace! amazing story – "I will send Mine only Son,"
> And the Lord Himself His glory veiled and came, the lowly One,

And creation donned her mourning, filled with wonderment to see
Man his mighty Maker spurning, slaying Him upon a tree.
Gaze thereon, my soul, and ponder o'er the ruin there expressed,
And confess in grateful wonder, by His dying thou art blessed.
Wondrous love! – all thought transcending – He Himself for me has given,
On this truth all else depending – 'Twas the Lord Himself from heaven.
(Frank Houghton)

Day 188

And do not forget to do good and to share with others, for with such sacrifices God is pleased. (Hebrews 13:16)

Daily reading: Deuteronomy 7

The term 'do-gooders' is often meant as an insult and sadly it's sometimes associated insincere and hypocritical Christians whose compassion in reality doesn't match their "Sunday profile." True Christians are to be 'do-gooders', not in a sentimental, self-righteous way, but in the truest sense of compassion. We follow the Master who 'went about doing good', and he didn't do that to be thanked or to be in the spotlight – nor was it inconsistent with who He really was as a Person. He dispensed good to the ungrateful, as well as the grateful – on one occasion at a ratio of nine to one! How closely does my 'doing' match that of the Saviour who put out His hand and touched?

Day 189

I am the song of the drunkards. (Psalm 69:12 RV)
I am become their song … I am a byword unto them.
(Job 30:9 RV)
I am their music. (Lamentations 3:63)

Daily reading: Deuteronomy 8

What did Job, David and Jeremiah have in common? All of them knew the hurt of being the subject of satirical songs sung by senseless men. In their drunken stupor, they mocked the messengers of God, forming words and fingering instruments like those 'that sing idle songs to the sound of the viol' (Amos 6.5 RV). It's even sadder that the great I AM, who said, 'I am the bread of life', 'I am the light of the world' and 'I am the way, the truth, and the life' could link His great Jehovah name to those deeply wounding words, 'I am become their song.' May He play on the cords of hearts that make melody in His presence, causing Him through higher themes to say, 'I AM their music.'

Day 190

Is the seed still in the barn? (Haggai 2:19)

Daily reading: Deuteronomy 9

Someone once said: 'If you keep your seed you'll lose it, if you sow it, you'll find it again.' It would be a strange farmer who, having bought expensive seed, kept it in his barn and never sowed it! It would stay single, instead of multiplying 30, 60 or 100-fold. What a waste! In the Lord's parable, seed is symbolic of the Word of God. Believers must sow the seed. The word of man can never take the place of the Word of God. Sadly, in some places today, the Bible's a closed book. In others, people clamour for it. Let's be diligent in teaching Scripture to those who don't read it for themselves and be keen to distribute both gospel and teaching content in print or electronically. Then, after sowing the seed, we must pray to the Lord of the harvest for a rich time of reaping because 'whoever sows generously will also reap generously.' (2 Cor.9:6).

> Eternal God, whose power upholds both flower and flaming star,
> To whom there is no here nor there, no time, nor near nor far,
> No alien race, no foreign shore, no child unsought, unknown,
> O send us forth, Thy prophets true, to make all lands Thine own!
> O God of righteousness and grace, seen in the Christ, Thy Son,
> Whose life and death reveal Thy face, by whom Thy will was done,
> Inspire Thy heralds of good news, to live Thy life divine,
> Till Christ is formed in all mankind and every land is Thine.
> (Lily Rendle)

Day 191

I strive always to keep my conscience clear [void of offence, RV] before God and man. (Acts 24:16)

Daily reading: Deuteronomy 10

Someone once described their conscience as 'a little three-cornered thing in here. When I do wrong it turns around and hurts very much. If I keep on doing wrong, it will turn until it wears the edges all off, and then it will not hurt anymore.' That's like Paul's description of some people whose consciences were 'seared with a hot iron' (1 Tim.4:2). Like the branded flesh of a beast, they no longer had the sense of feeling. How important it is to make sure that every wrong habit is abandoned, that our conscience is protected and preserved so that it might be 'void of offence', not void of feeling.

I want a principle within of watchful, godly fear,
A sensibility of sin, a pain to feel it near.
Help me the first approach to feel of pride or wrong desire;
To catch the wandering of my will, and quench the kindling fire.
From Thee that I no more may stray, no more Thy goodness grieve,
Grant me the filial awe, I pray, the tender conscience give.
Quick as the apple of an eye, O God, my conscience make!
Awake my soul when sin is nigh, and keep it still awake.
Almighty God of truth and love to me Thy power impart;
The burden from my soul remove, the hardness from my heart.
O may the least omission pain my reawakened soul,
And drive me to that blood again which makes the wounded whole.
(Charles Wesley)

Day 192

Canst thou bind the sweet influences of Pleiades, or loose the bands of Orion? (Job 38:31 KJV)

Daily reading: Deuteronomy 11

The word 'influence' occurs only once in the whole Bible, and it's here in a sublime passage in which the Almighty asks Job some unanswerable questions. The basic meaning of the word seems to be 'cluster.' It's known now that the stars in the constellation Pleiades, (anciently known as the 'seven sisters' although the telescope reveals many more stars in this group), are bound together gravitationally. The stars in the bright constellation Orion, on the other hand, are not bound together. Only God can either bind or release the stars, as He's the one who created them and placed them in the heavens. If the above interpretation is correct, isn't this verse remarkable evidence of the divine inspiration of scripture?

We sing the mighty power of God that made the mountains rise,
That spread the flowing seas abroad and built the lofty skies.
We sing the wisdom that ordained the sun to rule the day;
The moon shines full at his command, and all the stars obey.
(Isaac Watts)

Day 193

And the king said, "Let him return to his own house, but do not let him see my face." So Absalom returned to his own house, but did not see the king's face. (2 Samuel 14:24)

If you read the backstory, you'll see that David had figured out that Joab was behind the wise woman's charade. The point had been well made, but was there a grudging acceptance of Absalom's return by the king? Does the fact that Absalom wasn't permitted to see the king's face indicate that there was a half-heartedness about the king's recall? What we do know is that nothing of the kind applies to God's dealing with us. We shall see His face! In fact, God cared so deeply that He hid His own face from the Lord Jesus on the cross that we might see His face during glorious days of service to come.

Face to face with Christ, my Savior, face to face - what will it be
When with rapture I behold him, Jesus Christ who died for me?
Face to face I shall behold him, far beyond the starry sky;
Face to face in all his glory, I shall see him by and by.
(Carrie Ellis Breck)

Day 194

No one should seek their own good, but the good of others. (1 Corinthians 10:24)

Daily reading: Deuteronomy 13

Lord, help me to live from day to day in such a self-forgetful way
That even when I kneel to pray my prayers will be for others.
Help me in all the work I do to ever be sincere and true
And know that all I do for You must needs be done for others.
Let "self" be crucified and slain and buried deep;
And all in vain may efforts be to rise again unless to live for others.
And when my work on earth is done, and my new work in heaven's begun,
May I forget the crown I've won while thinking still of others.
Others, Lord, yes others! Let this my motto be:
Help me to live for others, That I may live like Thee.
(C.D. Meigs)

Day 195

"Bring the whole tithe into the storehouse, that there may be food in my house. Test me in this," says the Lord Almighty, "and see if I will not throw open the floodgates of heaven and pour out so much blessing that there will not be room enough to store it." (Malachi 3:10)

The Old Testament begins and ends with the floodgates of heaven. When they were opened in Genesis 7 earth's measureless outcome was the flood. In Malachi, they could have been opened again for the immeasurable blessing of God's people. All He wanted to see was their willingness to fill His storehouse with tithes and offerings from yielded lives. Are we robbing God? If so, we rob ourselves of the One Who "poured out His soul unto death" and now wants to "pour you out a blessing."

"There shall be showers of blessing": This is the promise of love;
There shall be seasons refreshing, sent from the Saviour above.
Showers of blessing, showers of blessing we need;
Mercy drops round us are falling, but for the showers we plead.
(D.W. Whittle)

Day 196

And he took bread, gave thanks and broke it, and gave it to them, saying, "This is my body given for you; do this in remembrance of me." (Luke 22:19)

Daily reading: Deuteronomy 15

In creation and in carpentry, in nature and in Nazareth, the Lord was the great Maker and Mender. He makes, we mar, and, in His skill and patience, He makes again. How disfigured the leper must have been; how complete his restoration. How broken the widow was until she met the Maker of stars and Mender of broken hearts (Ps.147:3,4). Why, then, this uncharacteristic act of breaking? In the hushed upper room we hear His own explanation – the loaf was symbolic of His body and the bruising He would shortly know. Broken for our mending!

The loaf He took spake of that frame,
Prepared by God for Him who came
To manifest His Father's name – Jesus our Lord.
(Charles Mann Luxmoore)

Day 197

... let your light shine before others, that they may see your good deeds and glorify your Father in heaven. (Matthew 5:16)

A serious condemnation of Christian living was expressed by a Buddhist in search of truth and light when he said, "I want to believe in Christ, but I have never seen Him in those who profess to follow Him." Dr. J. Stuart Holden once expressed his opinion that "the reason why the world does not know God is because it knows us so well." How sad if that's true!

> You are writing a gospel, a chapter each day,
> By deeds that you do, by words that you say,
> Men read what you write, whether faithless or true,
> So, what is the gospel according to you?
> (Author unknown)

Day 198

Love must be sincere. (Romans 12:9)

Daily reading: Deuteronomy 17

A young man spent an entire evening telling a girl how much he loved her with increasing dramatic passion. He said he couldn't live without her; that he'd go to the ends of the earth for her; yes, he'd go through fire for her, or gladly take a bullet for her. But as he was leaving he said to her, "I'll see you tomorrow night … well, that's if it's not raining." Hmm … how do you think that relationship turned out? How often we say we love God but deny it by our actions! "Dear children, let us not love with words or speech but with actions and in truth. This is how we know that we belong to the truth and how we set our hearts at rest in his presence" (1 Jn 3:18-19).

> We have not loved Thee as we ought,
> Nor cared that we are loved by Thee,
> Thy presence we have coldly sought,
> And feebly longed Thy face to see;
> Lord, give a pure and loving heart
> To feel and know Thee as Thou art.
> (T.B. Pollock)

Day 199

The kings of the earth set themselves, and the rulers take counsel together, against the Lord and against His Anointed … He who sits in the heavens shall laugh; The Lord shall hold them in derision. Then He shall speak to them in His wrath,

and distress them in His deep displeasure "Yet I have set My King on My holy hill of Zion." (Psalm 2:4-6 NKJV)

Daily reading: Deuteronomy 18

Could the contrast be any greater? We have the Adversary causing men to take a wrongful stand and God causing His Man to take His rightful seat. On one hand, we see men 'set' in their earthly threats: on the other, the Man 'set' on His heavenly throne. He is far beyond the reach of their feeble threats but will one day return to set up His kingdom for a thousand-year reign that will show how empty the claims of world powers – at whatever point in history - are.

> Jesus shall reign where'er the sun
> Doth his successive journeys run;
> His Kingdom stretch from shore to shore,
> Till moons shall wax and wane no more.
> Then come, O Lord, to earth again;
> Come, take Thy mighty power and reign;
> Bid tumults, wars and conflicts cease.
> Rule far and wide, Thou Prince of Peace.
> (Isaac Watts)

Day 200

... a dead person was being carried out—the only son of his mother, and she was a widow. When the Lord saw her, his heart went out to her and he said, "Don't cry." He said, "Young man, I say to you, get up!" (Luke 7:11,13)

Daily reading: Romans 1

To the onlookers, it was simply another dead person – to her it was her only son, both her heritage and her help. These were hot tears from a hurting heart. Bereavement had struck twice and tears of widowhood were coupled with tears of mourning motherhood. Death had spoken twice and inflicted its gloom, but the Life spoke twice to introduce His glory! At His word, her heart was supported and her tears stopped. He spoke again and she was surprised with joy. She was comforted, and death was conquered. And still He speaks, to turn the sadness of mourning into joy "in the morning."

> We expect a bright tomorrow - all will be well;
> Faith can sing through days of sorrow, all, all is well;
> On our Father's love relying, He our every need supplying,
> Or in living or in dying, all must be well.
> (Mrs. Peters)

Day 201

Greater love has no one than this: to lay down one's life for one's friends. (John 15:13)

Daily reading: Romans 2

Can you count me the leaves of the forest trees or the sand on the sea-washed shore, or the flowers bedecking the fragrant leas, or the grain in the harvest store? If you can, then I'll tell you His love to me who died for my sins on Calvary's tree. Can you count me the locks of glossy hair on the blooming, youthful head? Can you count me each particular star that shines when the day is sped? If you can, then I'll tell you His love to me who died for my sins on Calvary's tree. Can you count me the blades of grass that grow in the meadows all around, or the sparkling, glittering drops of dew at the sun's uprising found? But you cannot, and oh! I cannot tell the depths of His love to me who died for my sins on Calvary's tree (Fanny Crosby).

Day 202

Then Jesus told them, "You are going to have the light just a little while longer. Walk while you have the light, before darkness overtakes you. (John 12:35)

Daily reading: Romans 3

How important the words 'a little while' are. Keeping priorities in the correct order is a difficult task, and failure results in precious time being misused. That never happened with the Lord Jesus; he was never in the wrong place; and he never wasted a precious hour. Even mundane activities had a part in the great divine purposes reaching fulfilment before His disciples' eyes. How are we going to approach this day, this little while of extra opportunity? Let's review our plans in the light of His presence. 'Only one life, 'twill soon be past. Only what's done for Christ will last' (C.T. Studd).

A little while! our Lord shall come, and we shall wander here no more;
He'll take us to our Father's home, where He for us has gone before,
To dwell with Him, to see His face and sing the glories of His grace.
A little while, he'll come again; let us the precious hours redeem,
Our only grief to give him pain, our joy to serve and follow him.
(J.G. Deck)

Day 203

If I were hungry, I would not tell you. (Psalm 50:12)
Bring an offering and come into His courts. (Psalm 96:8)

Daily reading: Romans 4

If we had come to the altar with an animal sacrifice, we would have known that in our gift was "the food of the offering" (Lev.3.4,11) which God also described as 'My bread' (Ezek.44.7). It's no wonder He said, 'None shall appear before Me empty' (Ex.23.15). He longed to be satisfied and He still does. From all with which He's satisfied us in His Son, how can we not 'bring an offering', some fresh appreciation of Christ? How could we ever stand silently in His presence and not say something to satisfy the unspoken hunger of His heart?

O Lord, Thy courts we humbly tread, by thy best Spirit hither led,
We bring our sacrifice of praise, adoring Thee in grateful lays.
Great God, Thy love all love excels; it humbles us, yet praise compels!
Eternally our song shall be of Him who said, "Remember Me."
(J.B. Belton)

Day 204

The first thing Andrew did was to find his brother Simon and tell him, "We have found the Messiah" … And he brought him to Jesus. (John 1:40-42)

Daily reading: Romans 5

Those with relatives who haven't put faith in Christ long to be as effective as Andrew in personal witness. He'd followed Jesus, seen where He was living and spent time with Him (Jn 1:37-39). Have you followed, seen and stayed with Him long enough to be able to bring others?

Dear Saviour, how we long to win our loved ones all for Thee!
Yet oft our nearest kith and kin least yielding seem to be.
We intercede with anxious fears, yet still they turn away;
Lord, can it be, despite our tears that we obstruct Thy way?
Lord, help us pray and daily yield, and grant us soon to see
By Thine own saving truth revealed, our loved ones won for Thee.
(J. Sidlow Baxter)

Day 205

Jesus said to her, "I am the resurrection and the life. The one who believes in me will live, even though they die."
(John 11:25)
…we who are still alive and are left will be caught up together with them in the clouds to meet the Lord in the air. And so we will be with the Lord forever.
(1 Thessalonians 4:17)

Daily reading: Romans 6

Danton, a leader of the French Revolution, was on his way to the guillotine. He said to his companions on the scaffold, 'Our heads will meet in yonder sack.' That is the outlook on life if there is no resurrection of the dead. But because Christ is risen, and because the dead rise, the Christian believer as he lays the body of his beloved in the grave can say, 'Our souls will meet in yonder heaven.'

He comes! He comes! Oh, blest anticipation!
In keeping with His true and faithful word,
To call us to our heavenly consummation -
Caught up to be for ever with the Lord.
I am He that liveth, that liveth and was dead.
And behold! I am alive for evermore.
(C.R. Hurditch)

Day 206

In another battle with the Philistines at Gob, Elhanan … killed the brother of Goliath the Gittite. (2 Samuel 21:19)

Daily reading: Romans 7

The name Goliath means 'stripped, denuded, after the practice in war of stripping the vanquished.' We might scratch our heads as to why a parent would ever think of bestowing such a name on their offspring, but both Goliath and his brother had the thieving character which steals, kills and destroys (Jn 10:10). How often Satan displays the same ruthless tactics which ravages spiritual lives in their moment of weakness by means of a giant that should have been killed long ago. Elhanan means 'God is gracious.' If you're still plagued by a gigantic enemy, slay it today by the grace of God.

Yield not to temptation, for yielding is sin;
Each vict'ry will help you some other to win;
Fight valiantly onward, evil passions subdue;
Look ever to Jesus, He will carry you through.
Ask the Savior to help you, comfort, strengthen and keep you;
He is willing to aid you, He will carry you through.
(H.R. Palmer)

Day 207

When my life was ebbing away, I remembered you, Lord, and my prayer rose to you, to your holy temple. (Jonah 2:7)

Daily reading: Romans 8

Jonah 'went down' to Joppa to get away from the presence of the Lord, then he 'went down' into the ship for the same reason (1:3). When the sailors cast him overboard he went further down and, as the unhappy traveller inside the great fish, he went down to the very bottom of the mountains (2:6). Sometimes, we feel that we've also hit 'rock bottom.' The only way is up, and that's where we find God waiting for faith to replace fainting. It's then that we say, 'My prayer rose to You.' We come through One who knows about deep descent - he went 'down' from heaven to earth, from earth to Calvary, from Calvary to Hades and then, risen and exalted, now serves as our compassionate High Priest in the holy temple of the New Covenant.

Lord, let my prayer like incense rise, and when I lift my hands to Thee,
As on the evening sacrifice, look down from heaven well-pleased on me.
Mine eyes are unto Thee, my God! Behold me humbled in the dust;
I kiss the hand that wields the rod, I own thy chastisements are just.
But O! redeem me from the snares with which the world surrounds my feet,
Its riches, vanities, and cares, its love, its hatred, its deceit.
(James Montgomery)

Day 208

For who knows what is good for a person in life, during the few and meaningless days they pass through like a shadow. (Ecclesiastes 6:12)

At one point at least, Solomon seems to have had a jaded, cynical view of life. That shouldn't be the believer's perspective, but what are you making of yours? "To the preacher life's a sermon, to the joker it's a jest; to the miser life is money, to the loafer life is rest. To the lawyer life's a trial, to the poet life's a song, to the doctor life's a patient that needs treatment right along. To the soldier life's a battle, to the teacher life's a school; life's a good thing to the grafter, it's a failure to the fool. To the man upon the engine life's a long and heavy grade; it's a gamble to the gambler, to the merchant life is trade. Life is but a long vacation to the man who loves his work; life's an everlasting effort to shun duty, to the shirk; to the earnest, sincere worker life's a story ever new; life is what we try to make it—brother, what is life to you?" (S.E. Kiser)

Day 209

Now the battle became intense against Saul; and the archers hit him. (1 Samuel 31:3)

Daily reading: Romans 10

In Deuteronomy 20 God instructed that words of encouragement should be given by a priest to soldiers 'on the verge of battle.' Instead of visiting a priest before the battle of Mount Gilboa, Saul went to the medium at Endor. It's no wonder he lost the battle the next day! In our conflict as soldiers in the Lord's army, let's encourage one another. Is there a brother you know finding the battle intense or a sister who is struggling in the conflict? Will you strengthen your fellow-soldiers by words of encouragement and prayers? Will you help them to look to the great Victor, our Lord Jesus Christ?

Faint not, Christian, though the road leading to Thy blest abode
Darksome be and dangerous too,
Christ, thy Guide, will bring Thee through!
Faint not, Christian, though in rage Satan doth thy soul engage;
Take thee faith's anointed shield, bear it to the battlefield.
Faint not, Christian, though the world has its hostile flag unfurled;
Hold the cross of Jesus fast, Thou shall overcome at last!
(J.H. Evans)

Day 210

... for this very reason I came to this hour. (John 12:27)
... the hour had come for him to leave this world and go to the Father. (John 13:1)

The Lord's direction and destination were never in doubt. When in Gethsemane He anticipated Golgotha's deepest suffering, He declared, 'For this very reason I came to this hour.' Some went back (Jn 6:66), others went away (Jn 6:67), Peter went out (Lk.22:62), but the Lord 'went forward', 'went further' (Matt.26.39 RV). But Calvary wasn't the final goal. 'This hour' was also His hour 'to leave ... and go to the Father.' Praise God that He went on, not only through cornfields and towns and villages, but also 'through death' (Heb.2.14). Let's ensure that our worship is 'His hour' too.

Day 211

Then Judas ... said, 'Master, is it I'? (Matthew 26:25 NKJV)

Daily reading: Romans 12

No one can say, Jesus is Lord, except in the Holy Spirit (1 Cor.12:3). Eleven men said, 'Lord, is it I?' and Judas literally asked, 'Rabbi, is it I?'; each one was led by the Spirit to acknowledge His proper mastery and authority, except the betrayer who was unable to utter such a word. Led by a devilish impulse to deliver Him up, he left the Saviour's side in the upper room, only to meet Him in the garden where he repeated that empty word, 'Rabbi, Rabbi' which may haunt him for eternity. Is Jesus just a good teacher to you, or is he the Lord of your life?

Jesus, Master, whose I am, purchased thine alone to be
By thy blood, O spotless Lamb, shed so willingly for me,
Let my heart be all thine own, let me live to thee alone.
Lord, thou needest not, I know, service such as I can bring;
Yet I long to prove and show full allegiance to my King.
Thou an honor art to me: let me be a praise to thee.
(Frances Ridley Havergal)

Day 212

Lazy hands make for poverty, but diligent hands bring wealth. (Proverbs 10:4)

Daily reading: Romans 13

A stranger was passing along a road and uncertain of his way when he saw a shepherd boy lying by the roadside while the sheep were grazing contentedly in nearby pastures. Approaching the boy, the stranger asked the way. The boy, scarcely looking up, stretched out his arm nonchalantly and said, 'That way.'

While grateful, the stranger was a little irked by the casualness and decided to make a point. 'My lad, if you can show me anything lazier than that, I'll give you a pound.' Without looking up, the lad said, 'Put it in my pocket.' It's a rare exception that proves the rule, because under normal circumstances it doesn't pay to be lazy! God definitely doesn't reward laziness, but he does bless whole-heartedness. Let's be known for the latter.

> Zeal is that pure and heav'nly flame, the fire of love supplies;
> While that which often bears the name, is self in a disguise.
> Self may its poor reward obtain, and be applauded here;
> But zeal the best applause will gain, when Jesus shall appear.
> Dear Lord, the idol self dethrone, and from our hearts remove;
> And let no zeal by us be shown, but that which springs from love.
> (John Newton)

Day 213

Comfort, comfort my people, says your God. (Isaiah 40:1)
I, even I, am he who comforts you. (Isaiah 51:12)
As a mother comforts her child, so will I comfort you ... (Isaiah 66:13)

Daily reading: Romans 14

'Three precious pillows to rest your head on', was the way one sick visitor described these texts to his bed-ridden friend. Whichever way you look at them, they are wonderful promises from the God of all comfort. The Hebrew word for comfort itself is full of suggestiveness, coming from a root which carries the thought of 'breathing deeply,' as though comfort carries with it a display of one's feelings. And it does, for God's comfort flows out of His compassion and reaches deep into our hearts in its warmth and tenderness. 'As a mother comforts her child' - what could be more tender than that? Whatever your need, won't you rest your head on these promises today?

> When I get weary with toils of the day, off in the secret I kneel and pray;
> There I can hear my Lord sweetly say, "Come closer, my child, to me."
> When in afflictions I suffer long, Jesus comes bringing this lovely song:
> "Trust in my grace, and you shall be strong, "Come closer, my child, to me."
> When I am meeting with trials severe,
> When I am parting with loved ones here,
> Looking to Jesus, His voice I can hear:
> "Come closer, my child, to me."
> (Barney E. Warren)

Day 214

Philip answered him, "It would take more than half a year's wages to buy enough bread for each one to have a bite!" (John 6:7)

Daily reading: Romans 15

It was quite an impressive display of mental arithmetic and impromptu event planning from Philip! But he'd reckoned without the Lord who could transcend the rules of mathematics by taking 2 and 5 and multiplying them into 5000. Commanding the multitude to recline, the Lord gave thanks and filled each with multiple bites of bread and fish. Doubtless Philip, too, was a beneficiary! Empty wallets didn't need to equal empty baskets. Let us learn with Philip that *'The great Creator became my Saviour, And all God's fullness dwelleth in Him.'*

All things living He doth feed; His full hand supplies their need:
For His mercies shall endure, ever faithful, ever sure.
(John Milton)

Day 215

Some trust in chariots and some in horses, but we trust in the name of the Lord our God. (Psalm 20:7)

Daily reading: Romans 16

Leaving all with Jesus, heart and mind at rest; for whate'er betideth, Jesus knoweth best. Though no ray of sunshine o'er my path is shed, soon the mists will vanish and the night have fled. Leaving all with Jesus, though I may not see, for the length'ning shadows that encompass me. Darkness radiant seemeth, shadows disappear; joy effaces sorrow when my Lord is near. Leaving all with Jesus, striving to be pure; strong in Him enduring, though the world allure. Trusting, yet hard striving wrong thoughts to subdue, through Him overcoming all that is not true. Leaving all with Jesus, leaning on His might; prayerful, watchful, anxious to be led aright. There's no time for sighing, resting on His Word; all in all is Jesus, trusted and adored. (E. Middleton)

Day 216

... if you lay the foundation and are not able to finish it, everyone who sees it will ridicule you, saying, 'This person began to build and wasn't able to finish.' (Luke 14:29-30)

Over 350 years ago a shipload of travellers landed on the northeast coast of America. The first year they established a town site. The next year they elected a town government. The third year the town government planned to build a road five miles westward into the wilderness. In the fourth year the people tried to impeach their town government because they thought it was a waste of public funds to build a road five miles westward into a wilderness. Who needed to go there anyway? Here were people who had the vision to see three thousand miles across an ocean and overcome great hardships to get there. But in just a few years they were not able to see even five miles out of town. They had lost their pioneering vision. With a clear vision of what we can become in Christ, no ocean of difficulty is too great. Without it, we rarely move beyond our current boundaries (L. Anderson).

Day 217

The soldiers twisted together a crown of thorns and put it on his head. They clothed him in a purple robe. (John 19:2)

Daily reading: Jonah 1

And He let them. They were cut down from the cursed earth at their feet; thorns vindictively interwoven by the hands of sinners and thrust on His head as others bowed in mockery. Earth's lowest for heaven's Highest. But it's different now! The Lord of glory has been cut off from the land of the living and many bow at His feet with thoughts, victoriously interwoven by the hands of saints, to place them in His hands. And He lets them!

> A crown of thorns for Him is made,
> He 'neath the curse doth bleed;
> In purple robe He stands arrayed –
> He holds the mocking reed.
> (Author unknown)

Day 218

As the shepherd taketh out of the mouth of the lion two legs, or a piece of an ear; so shall the children of Israel be taken out. (Amos 3:12 RV)

Daily reading: Jonah 2

Some people go to great lengths to explain why they can't do something; others just get on with it and do what they can. By the time the sheep was in the lion's mouth, the chance of the shepherd saving its life was surely gone. But, because of his integrity and sense of responsibility he did what he could. Perhaps all he could sorrowfully take back as evidence of his brave attempts would be a piece of an ear. Have we given up trying to rescue someone from the clutches of sin, believing that they're a lost cause? God is still able to deprive the lion of his meal!

Day 219

The Lord gave them rest on every side, just as he had sworn to their ancestors. Not one of their enemies withstood them ... Not one of all the Lord's good promises to Israel failed; every one was fulfilled. (Joshua 21:44-45)

Daily reading: Jonah 3

The child sat by the road bawling loudly. A passer-by asked him what the matter was. "My ma, she's gone and drowned the kittens," the boy wailed. "Oh, isn't that too bad!" was the sympathetic response. The child bawled the louder. "An' ma she promised me that I could drown 'em." What could the response be to that? Yes, it hurts when promises are broken - even very bad ones! How thankful we are that all God's promises are good and that He always keeps them. Only one response:

> Standing on the promises of Christ, my King,
> Through eternal ages let his praises ring;
> Glory in the highest, I will shout and sing,
> Standing on the promises of God.
> Standing on the promises that cannot fail.
> When the howling storms of doubt and fear assail,
> By the living Word of God I shall prevail,
> Standing on the promises of God.
> (Russell Kelso Carter)

Day 220

... here we do not have an enduring city. (Hebrews 13:14)
... what is seen is temporary. (2 Corinthians 4:18)
I press on toward the goal ... the prize. (Philippians 3:14)

Daily reading: Jonah 4

Are you a peripatetic Christian? You should be because it describes a believer on the move! It's an apt description of Paul, isn't it? There was so much to be done and every minute was valuable. Writing, preaching, praying, counselling, exhorting, encouraging, travelling. He didn't own a house, and his address was a moving target. He might be found in prison, or with Priscilla and Aquila, or even aboard ship. Paul urgently lived life to the full and time was important to him. With satisfaction he wrote, 'I have finished the race ... I have kept the faith' (2 Tim.4:7). His voice became silent, his quill pen dried out, his travels over, his destination reached - at home with the Lord. What a journey! What a Saviour!

Oft in danger, oft in woe, onward Christian, onward go!
Bear the toil, maintain the strife, strengthened with the bread of life.
Let not sorrow dim your eye, soon shall every tear be dry;
Let not fear your course impede, great your strength, if great your need.
Onward then to glory move, more than conquerors may ye prove;
Though opposed by many a foe, onward Christians, onward go!
(F.S. Colquhoun)

Day 221

I am full of tossings. (Job 7:4)

Daily reading: Micah 1

The Lord knows all about your sleepless tossing and turning and he understands that your restlessness reflects the rollings of your mind. It makes for a long night, doesn't it, when unresolved problems weigh so heavily that sleep flees and your whole being seems to be in a flap? Just remember, He's awake too. Tell Him. Let Him ease your turmoil and let Him help you face the dawning of the day.

I will fling wide a door of hope; the past shall drop away;
The shackles shall be broken, and the wounds that bleed today
Shall be as though they never were; beneath My healing touch
The pain that bars the gate of sleep shall loose its evil clutch.
(Nora Hanssen)

Day 222

... by their fruit you will recognize them.
(Matthew 7:20)

The Master came to the fig tree and saw the foliage there
Of thick and shady branches, To hungry eyes so fair.
But He found that it was barren and bore no luscious fruit,
For life was gone, and very soon 'twas withered to the root.
The Master came to the Temple and saw the worship there,
The riches and the customs, to Jewish eyes so fair;
But to Him 'twas all corruption, His house a den of thieves,
And all its boasted glory was fruitless, only leaves
The Master comes to our fireside and sees the family there
And one goes off to the pictures, another to Vanity Fair.
For, instead of family worship and intercessory prayer
The saints are torn to pieces, their failings all laid bare.
The Master to the assembly Has come! What sees He here?
The busy round of service and meetings held so dear.
But He sees the strife and divisions, and His Holy Spirit grieves
To find that many efforts are fruitless - mostly leaves.
(Jessie Brown Pounds)

Day 223

The night is nearly over; the day is almost here. So let us put aside the deeds of darkness and put on the armour of light. (Romans 13:12)

Daily reading: Micah 3

This is common sense because of course the armour of light won't fit while we're still wearing the deeds of darkness! We can't cover up our wrong thoughts with the helmet of salvation; instead we need to have the mind of Christ. We mustn't protect an evil heart of unbelief; we need to have it changed to a true heart that operates in fulness of faith. How prone we are to try to fight Christian battles with the wrong equipment, and sadly sometimes even with the wrong motives. If we recognize the awful, spiritual nature of our enemy, we'll realize our need for the spiritual armour God's prepared for us. And if we haven't even put that armour on, we shouldn't be anticipating that today will be a day of victory, should we?

Put on the armor of our God, be strong to do His will;
Dare not go forth for once unarmed, thy foes would do thee ill.
Put on the armor; girt with truth, the work is not thine own;
Bind to thy heart the law of God, fulfilled by Christ alone.
Put on the armor; shod with peace thy feet shall firm endure;

Though snares beset and thorns may pierce, He makes thy footsteps sure.
Put on the armor, take thy shield, faith in the risen Lord:
Once pierced with darts still aimed at thee, He conquers with a word.
(E.C. Ellsworth)

Day 224

Stephen ... saw ... Jesus standing. (Acts 7:55)
I sink ... where there is no standing. (Psalm 69:2 NKJV)
I saw a Lamb ... standing at the centre. (Revelation 5:6)

Daily reading: Micah 4

The Lord stood under an oak tree while Gideon offered a sacrifice (Jud.6:19). He stood among the myrtle trees to tell Zechariah of impending judgment (Zech.1:11,12). He stood beneath a sycamore tree on His way to be sacrificed (Luke 19:4,5). Watching over weary disciples, He stood among olive trees as the clouds of His impending judgment thickened (Mat.26:45). He didn't go to Calvary to stand under a tree but to be crucified upon it. On it, He went through the turbulence of judgment and sacrifice in the place where there was no standing, so that we can stand in the presence of God.

And then in dark Gethsemane, beneath the shady olive tree, prostrate in soul agony - He was there. And oh, my soul! I see Him now, a crown of thorns upon His brow: creation groans and wonders how - He was there (Mrs. McKendrick).

Day 225

One of the servant girls ... saw Peter ... "I don't know or
understand what you're talking about," he said.
(Mark 14:66-69)

Daily reading: Micah 5

When the Lord wanted quiet acquiescence, Peter was quick to wield his sword (Jn 18.10). Now, when quick defence was needed, he was as clumsy with his words as he'd been with his weapon. It's recorded for our spiritual well-being that the man who'd wrapped himself and warmed himself (Mark 14:51,67), didn't respond to his Master's advice to watch (Mark 14:38). What kind of message do we give by our actions and words? Shouldn't we watch our steps, because everyone else is!

We are the only Bible the careless world will read;
We are the sinner's gospel, we are the scoffer's creed;
We are the Lord's last message given in deed and word.
What if the type is crooked? What if the print is blurred?
(Annie Johnson Flint)

Day 226

Be perfect, therefore, as your heavenly Father is perfect.
(Matthew 5:48)

Daily reading: Micah 6

The fact that his two pet bantam hens laid very small eggs troubled little
Johnny. At last he was seized with inspiration. Johnny's father, upon going to
the fowl-run one morning, was surprised to see an ostrich egg tied to one of
the beams, with this exhortation chalked above it: "Keep your eye on this and
do your best." It was probably just as well that the hens couldn't read, because
otherwise they would have felt pretty intimidated! We might feel equally
intimidated by reading the commandments of Jesus and the exhortations of
Paul, Peter and others. How can we possibly reach the level of perfection of
Matthew 5:48? It helps when we understand that the word is translated as
'mature' in other verses. 'Maturity' can only come over time and for humans
it's a gradual accumulation of learning from life's little and often mundane
events and circumstances. Keep your eyes on Christ…

Day 227

Some will say, 'I belong to the Lord.' (Isaiah 44:5)
For to me, to live is Christ and to die is gain. (Philippians 1:21)
Demas, because he loved this world, has deserted me and has
gone to Thessalonica. (2 Timothy 4:10)

Daily reading: Micah 7

The use of the word 'turncoat' for a deserter is said to come from the American
Civil War. One man had the colours of the North on one side of his jacket and
the South on the other, wearing it whichever way suited him best at the time!
Is it obvious to people whose side you are on, or do you change allegiance
when things look bad?

We're marching to Canaan with banner and song,
We're soldiers enlisted to fight 'gainst the wrong;
But lest in the conflict our strength should divide

We ask "Who among us is on the Lord's side?"
The sword may be burnished, the armour be bright
(E'en Satan appears as an angel of light)
Yet darkly the bosom may treachery hide,
While lips are professing, "I'm on the Lord's side."
Oh, who is there among us, the true and the tried,
Who'll stand by his colours, who's on the Lord's side?
(Paulina)

Day 228

"Is there any word from the LORD?" "Yes, Jeremiah replied." (Jeremiah 37:17)

Daily reading: Genesis 1

There always is a word from the Lord if we're prepared to receive it. King Zedekiah wasn't prepared and he didn't want anyone to know he was enquiring; so he sent his message secretly. But he knew enough about the Lord to realize that His word doesn't change. God had a message for him and if he'd listened he would have been spared a lot of anguish. Are you in some kind of dilemma? Is there some sort of crisis in your life? Do you have a big decision to be made, perhaps? There's a word from the Lord for you. Wait for it and as you do so pray:

Master, speak; though least and lowest let me not unheard depart,
Master, speak; for oh, Thou knowest all the yearning of my heart!
Knowest all its truest need: speak and make me blest indeed.
Master, speak, and make me ready when Thy voice is truly heard,
With obedience glad and steady still to follow every word.
I am listening, Lord, for Thee - what hast Thou to say to me?
(Frances Ridley Havergal)

Day 229

It is the Lord your God you must follow, and him you must revere. Keep his commands and obey him; serve him and hold fast to him. (Deuteronomy 13:4)

Daily reading: Genesis 2

I'll follow Thee, and step by step along the track I'll walk;
Believing that Thy promises shall never come to nought;
Jehovah-Shantmah, blessed Name, whate'er the danger be,
Thy promise is salvation sure, and Thine the victory.
The Lord of hosts my refuge is, Jehovah-nissi too.
Jehovah-jireh as my God provides the journey through;
I trust Thee, simply trust Thee, lay my troubled fears to rest:
I follow where Thou leadest, for my Father knoweth best.
(E. Rowa)

Day 230

**Zion, which is desolate, the foxes walk upon it.
(Lamentations 5:18)
Take us the foxes, the little foxes, that spoil the vines.
(Song of Solomon 2:15)**

Daily reading: Genesis 3

Have you ever noticed that foxes rarely walk? They're constantly on the alert and ready to run as soon as they sense danger. Zion, great place of God's holiness, didn't your foxes sense any threat? No, they were at ease because your people were at ease. In the place where God was homeless, the foxes felt at home. It's like that with sin as well. The Devil flees when resisted, but too often he's allowed to prowl around in areas where holiness should have kept him out. Where is he walking in your life?

And yet - O sad confession! I am so prone to sin
That even in those holy times forbidden thoughts creep in,
And as the little foxes the tender vines destroy,
These little sins if unconfessed soon steal away our joy.
(William Blane)

Day 231

**I remember my affliction and my wandering, the bitterness and
the gall. I well remember them ... (Lamentations 3:19,20)**

Daily reading: Genesis 4

This is the comment that adds great poignancy to an already poignant gathering. As we remember Him, we are to contemplate that the Man on the garden floor, who faced Calvary because of the joy that was set before Him, is now the Man on the throne with perfect recollection of the sufferings that are behind Him. If He remembers, how can we forget?

Gethsemane, can I forget or there Thy conflict see,
Thine agony and blood-like sweat, and not remember Thee?
When to the cross I turn mine eyes and rest on Calvary,
O Lamb of God, my sacrifice, I must remember Thee-
Remember Thee and all Thy pains and all Thy love to me;
Yea, while a breath, a pulse remains, I will remember Thee.
(James Montgomery)

Day 232

I was strengthened as the hand of the Lord my God was upon me. (Ezra 7:28)

Daily reading: Genesis 5

It was a large and daunting work that Ezra had undertaken and he needed strength. But in the simple language of his heart the hand of God was upon him and this was all he needed to strengthen him. A veteran soldier was ordered by the Duke of Wellington to win a difficult position in the battle. He turned to the Duke and said, 'I will go, sir; but first give me a grip of your conquering hand.' Are you going? Are you gripping?

Trust thou in God, in secret to Him pray,
Trust thou in God, He'll be thy strength and stay;
Trust thou in God, make Him thy dearest friend,
Trust thou in God, He'll keep thee to the end.
(J. Robertson)

Day 233

He is the Lord; let him do what is good in his eyes. (1 Samuel 3:18)

Daily reading: Genesis 6

Although they'd both been struck with unforeseen injury and illness, the couple stressed their trust in the Lord, searching for His purpose in their suffering. 'Perhaps we shall be more Christlike. We remember what the old widow in the church here used to say cheerfully with every fresh trial, "I must take an awful lot of shaping!"' Those who knew the old lady recognised her godly meekness.

She had prayed to be made like her Saviour,
And the burdens He gave her to bear
Had been but the great Sculptor's teaching
To help answer her earnest prayer.
(Author unknown)

Day 234

The love of Christ constrains us ... that those who live should live no longer for themselves, but for Him who died for them and rose again. (2 Corinthians 5:14,15 RV)

Daily reading: Genesis 7

The love of Christ constrains us, or it should do! The same word is used when Simon's mother-in-law was 'holden with a great fever' (Lk.4:38 RV). It gripped her and held her fast to her bed, as fevers have a habit of doing. How good it is when the love of Christ so grips our hearts that we're held fast to Him and we no longer live for ourselves. Then we'll be able to meaningfully sing:

Were the whole realm of nature mine,
That were an offering far too small;
Love so amazing, so divine,
Demands my heart, my life, my all.
(Isaac Watts)

Day 235

Mary ... sat at the Lord's feet listening to what he said. (Luke 10:39)
... a woman came to him with an alabaster jar of very expensive perfume, which she poured on his head. (Matthew 26:7)

Daily reading: Genesis 8

We mustn't confuse activity with achievement. While Martha served, Mary sat. She chose the 'good part.' Martha knew increasing agitation but Mary knew growing inspiration! Was it at His feet that she learned about His burial? The 'good part' (Lk.10:42) of attention became the 'good work' (Matt.26:10) of anointing.

'Twas sitting at His feet she heard,
And from His lips drank in His word
Until her very soul was stirred - for Jesus.
Wouldst thou like her a 'good work' do,
Thou first must choose the 'good part' too,
And learn the heart so deep, so true - of Jesus.
(C. Thompson)

Day 236

You show that you are a letter from Christ ... written not with ink but with the Spirit of the living God, not on tablets of stone but on tablets of human hearts. (2 Corinthians 3:3)

Daily reading: Genesis 9

Do not say your influence is confined to a narrow sphere. Yon little candle is not a sun; yet observe how bright it shines, how far it spreads its rays in the dark night! Hide not then your light, whatever it be, under a bushel; nor keep your talent, because it is a single one, wrapped up in a napkin. Of this I can assure you, that if you adorn the Gospel by a holy conversation, you will give light to some who sit in darkness, and prove a blessing to your relations, friends, and neighbors. You will preach to the eyes what we preach to the ears. You will be living epistles known and read of all men. (E. Ward)

Day 237

Stay close to the king wherever he goes. (2 Chronicles 23:7)

Daily reading: Genesis 10

These were difficult and dangerous days for the young king to come to the throne. It called for determination (v.3), discipline (vv.4-6) and devotion to duty (v.8), initiated and constantly supported by Jehoiada, the priest. Ittai, whose name means near, had faced a similar challenge to be true to his name and stay close to his king, David. Can the Lord count on your constant companionship? Will you promise to be close to the King, wherever he goes?

Thou hast called me to Thee, Master! Thou hast bid me follow Thee.
And I long to do Thy bidding, till Thy face in light I see.
But in nature's strength no longer, Thou alone my strength must be;
When on Thee my weakness leaneth, then Thy power rests on me.
(C. Thompson)

Day 238

"Do not touch my anointed ones; do my prophets no harm."
(Psalm 105:15)
God anointed Jesus of Nazareth with the Holy Spirit and power
… they killed him by hanging him on a cross. (Acts 10:38,39)

Daily reading: Genesis 11

The sign said 'DO NOT TOUCH', yet, through long centuries of shame, the patient Son of God looked on as a long line of anointed men were abused with "jeers and flogging, and even chains and imprisonment. They were put to death by stoning; they were sawed in two; they were killed by the sword. They went about … destitute, persecuted and mistreated—" (Heb.11:36,37). In every case, He saw God's command being ignored. Then He stepped into humanity: not just an anointed man, but the Messiah; not just a man with the prophetic word, but the Word - and how brutally they touched God's Anointed, how badly they harmed His Prophet.

> Nailed upon Golgotha's tree, faint and bleeding, who is He?
> Hands and feet so rudely torn, wreathed with crown of twisted thorn.
> Once He lived in heaven above, happy in His Father's love,
> Son of God, tis He, tis He, nailed upon Gologatha's tree.
> (based on a hymn by Dr. H.H. Milman)

Day 239

If others have this right of support from you, shouldn't we have
it all the more? But we did not use this right. On the contrary,
we put up with anything rather than hinder the gospel of
Christ. (1 Corinthians 9:12)

Daily reading: Genesis 12

Maybe Paul expected more in return from the Corinthians, but his zeal and love meant he'd put up with anything, including their attitude and his many other afflictions, rather than the preaching of the gospel be hindered. What a lot must be hidden behind that word 'anything'! Is anything deterring or discouraging you today? Is the response disappointing from those you've tried to serve? May God give you the grace to put up with anything for Christ's sake.

What wouldst Thou have me to do, Lord?
Whatever it may be,
Though mine is a weak and trembling hand,
I'm willing to do at Thy command
Anything, Lord, for Thee.
Where wouldst Thou have me to go, Lord?
Wherever it may be,
My feet Thou hast placed on the King's highway,
Thy grace doth enable me to say,
Anywhere, Lord, for Thee.
What wouldst Thou have me to yield, Lord?
Whatever it may be,
All, all that I have and am is Thine,
And willingly, gladly I resign
Ev'rything, Lord, for Thee.
(E.E. Williams)

Day 240

You open your hand and satisfy the desires of every living thing. (Psalm 145:16)
I give them eternal life, and they shall never perish; no one will snatch them out of my hand. (John 10:28)

Daily reading: Genesis 13

'Take a handful of cherries', said a kind greengrocer to a little boy out shopping with his mum. When the boy hesitated, the shopkeeper dipped his own hand into the basket and gave him a liberal helping of the luscious fruit. 'Why didn't you help yourself when he asked you?' asked his mum outside. "Cos his hand was bigger than mine!' the boy replied innocently. God's hand is bigger than ours, much bigger! So big, in fact, it supplies the need of every living thing. It's a mighty hand (1 Pet.5:6), a secure, protecting hand. How comforting to remember that our times are in His hand!

Our times are in Your hand; O God, we wish them there!
Our lives, our souls, our all we leave entirely to Your care.
Our times are in Your hand whatever they may be,
Pleasing or painful, dark or bright, as best may seem to Thee.
Our times are in Your hand; why should we doubt or fear?
The Father's hand will never cause His child a needless tear.
Our times are in Your hand, we'd always trust in Thee
Till we, in yonder heavenly land, Thyself in glory see.
(William Freeman Lloyd)

Day 241

**... be of good cheer; your sins are forgiven you.
(Matthew 9:2 NKJV)
Be of good cheer! It is I; do not be afraid.
(Matthew 14:27 NKJV)
Be of good cheer, Paul; for ... you must also bear
witness at Rome. (Acts 23:11 NKJV)**

Daily reading: Genesis 14

We're guilty of encouraging with platitudes at times. Job's comforters might have said to the palsied man, 'Don't worry, things might improve.' What a waste of words! To other sufferers in the storm, Paul encouraged positively, 'Be of good cheer,' (Acts 27:22 NKJV) because he'd proved these words during the ominous time of his arrest by the authorities. It should be the same with us. As we benefit from life's experiences, let's encourage and benefit each other. Experience with Him eliminates empty words from our vocabulary. Accentuate the positive - "be of good cheer"!

> Be of good cheer, the Lord of hosts will surely help your case,
> Freely He came and paid the debt to save the human race.
> Be of good cheer, fear not, fear not, have faith in Heaven's love;
> God will not leave the trusting soul, but will a helper prove.
> Be of good cheer, be strong, be strong, let nothing make you fear;
> Just keep your spirit full of song, and watching unto prayer.
> (Charles Price Jones)

Day 242

But about the Son he says, "Your throne, O God, will last for ever and ever; a scepter of justice will be the scepter of your kingdom. You have loved righteousness and hated wickedness; therefore God, your God, has set you above your companions by anointing you with the oil of joy." (Hebrews 1:8-9)

Daily reading: Genesis 15

In Old Testament times, as well as being an important source of light, oil was used to anoint the bridegroom at his wedding, the priest at his consecration and the king at his coronation. Oil was obviously a sign of privilege, purity and joy – all things associated with the work of the Holy Spirit. What joy must be in the heart of God as He looks upon His incomparable Son, whose purity as a Man wasn't shown simply by an adherence to righteous rules but a Spirit-led life demonstrating a love of righteousness. How much we need the Holy Spirit to live like Him.

Our blest Redeemer, ere He breathed His tender, last farewell,
A Guide, a Comforter bequeathed with us to dwell.
And every virtue we possess, and every victory won,
And every thought of holiness are His alone.
Spirit of purity and grace, our weakness pitying see;
Oh, make our hearts Thy dwelling place, and worthier Thee.
(Harrier Auber)

Day 243

Now that you have purified yourselves by obeying the truth so that you have sincere love for each other, love one another deeply, from the heart. (1 Peter 1:22)

Daily reading: Genesis 16

I would be true, for there are those who trust me;
I would be pure, for there are those who care;
I would be strong, for there is much to suffer;
I would be brave, for there is much to dare.
I would be friend of all—the foe, the friendless;
I would be giving, and forget the gift;
I would be humble, for I know my weakness;
I would look up, and laugh, and love, and lift. Amen.
(Howard A. Walter)

Day 244

"Why wasn't this perfume sold and the money given to the poor? It was worth a year's wages ...you will not always have me ..." (John 12:5,8)

Daily reading: Genesis 17

Another week of work. Another payslip showing its evaluation by an employer. How will its earnings be used? Perhaps it presents an opportunity to do good to the ever-present poor. Some will be needed for the current demands of home and family; some can be stored away to meet a future need. The ointment was most likely gradually saved, for as Judas pointed out its value was equivalent to almost a year's wages. He knew the cost of everything but the value of nothing. Mary spent well when the day of opportunity came. Is the Lord still waiting for us to recognize His worth?

> The box, unbroken, could have kept its treasure
> And pleased the fancy of a dinner guest;
> But Mary broke the box, and in the breaking,
> Her Lord, and all the world beside, were blest.
> (William R. Newell)

Day 245

In the sweat of your face you shall eat bread.
(Genesis 3:19 NKJV)
I am the bread of life. (John 6:35)
… and his sweat was like drops of blood falling to the ground.
(Luke 22:44)

Daily reading: Genesis 18

There were no bread-makers in the garden. Bread and sweat went together outside Eden's place of broken communion with God. For a loaf to be made in the outside place there had to be the toil of ploughing, sowing, watering, weeding, harvesting, grinding, kneading and baking. It was sweat in the field, and more sweat at the fire. We remember that when the Bread of Life came He knew the toil of the outside place and went through the sweat of the field and the fire that we might feed upon Him in unbroken communion.

> For me it was in the garden He prayed, "Not My will, but Thine."
> He had no tears for His own griefs, but sweat-drops of blood for mine.
> He took my sins and my sorrows, He made them His very own.
> He bore the burden to Calv'ry and suffered and died alone.
> (Charles H. Gabriel)

Day 246

Let her alone; for her soul is in deep distress, and the LORD has hidden it from me. (2 Kings 4:27)

The woman was in pieces because she'd suffered the loss of someone she loved. Nothing could ease what she was going through, and there were really no words that could bring sympathy or help in trying to accept the situation. She had to get in contact with God, so she sought out Elisha. He gave her space to unload the problem with all its frustration and bitterness. Perhaps today or this week you might be asked just to listen to someone pouring out their hurt and grief. Be like Elisha. Take time to be with them. You may not understand, but you can listen and give them your support. And you can help them to seek out God.

Help us to help each other, Lord, each other's cross to bear;
Let each his friendly aid afford, and feel another's care.
Up into thee, our living head, let us in all things grow,
And by thy sacrifice be led the fruits of love to show.
Touched by the lodestone of thy love let all our hearts agree;
And ever towards each other move, and ever move towards thee.
This is the bond of perfectness, thy spotless charity.
O let us still, we pray, possess the mind that was in thee.
(Charles Wesley)

Day 247

... we wait for the blessed hope—the appearing of the glory of our great God and Saviour, Jesus Christ, who gave himself for us to redeem us ... (Titus 2:13-14)

Daily reading: Genesis 20

Hortense - the daughter of Napoleon's Josephine and the mother of Napoleon III - wrote to her son when he was in America for a short time. He was seriously ill, and she didn't expect to meet him again in this life. But she wrote: "Believe that certainly we shall meet again. Have faith in this consoling idea. It is too necessary not to be true." This sounds like faith based on human reasoning or simply wishful thinking. Thankfully, we have something far more solid to base our hopes on than an idea!

Our Lord's coming draweth nigh, His long-sought unveiling;
Let us Maranatha cry with a faith unfailing!
At the moment of His choice God's great might displaying,
He will make His saints rejoice, Christ is not delaying.
Gathering cloud and threat of sea home the traveller urges;

We would to the haven flee where storm no more surges.
In our hearts the breaking dawn hope anew awakens,
And the day-star with the morn entrance sure betokens.
(G. Nelson)

Day 248

I die daily. (1 Corinthians 15:31 NKJV)

Daily reading: Genesis 21

In earlier life Jacob had lived up to a name that means supplanter (someone who takes the place of someone else.) By self-assertion, he'd ousted his brother Esau (Gen.27:35) and his father-in-law Laban (Gen.30:42,43) from the place of blessing. But Jabbok (which means empty) was a turning point for Jacob as the divine Wrestler announced, 'no more Jacob' (Gen.32:28). Paul, too, appreciated that in Christian experience dying precedes living. Self had been crucified, as He explained, "I no longer live, but Christ …" (Gal.2:20). Will you die today so that Christ may live in you?

There is no other pathway if thou wouldst really be
Conformed unto the image of Him who died for thee.
Thou canst not be like Jesus till self is crucified:
And as a daily process the cross must be applied.
(J. Danson Smith)

Day 249

But the LORD came down to see the city. (Genesis 11:5)
… I will go down and see. (Genesis 18:21)
I have come down to rescue them. (Exodus 3:8)

Daily reading: Genesis 22

The Lord came down, but did anyone notice? Or was God at Babel without anyone sensing His presence? Was it any different at Sodom and Gomorrah? No, it wasn't and how sad to be oblivious to such a Visitor! Unchanged in His purpose, He came down again, and this time they knew. Why? because He finally revealed Himself in the lamb (Exodus 12). Like them, we also know He came down, and the Lamb has brought us to love the presence of the descending and condescending God.

Rejoice and be glad! The Redeemer hath come!
Go, look on His cradle, His cross and His tomb.
Rejoice and be glad! For the blood hath been shed;
Redemption is finished, the price hath been paid.
Rejoice and be glad! For the lamb who was slain
O'er death is triumphant and liveth again!
(Horatius Bonar)

Day 250

They claim to know God, but by their actions they deny him. They are detestable, disobedient and unfit for doing anything good. (Titus 1:16)

Daily reading: Genesis 23

You tell on yourself by the friends you seek, by the very manner in which you speak, by the way you employ your leisure time, by the use you make of dollar and dime. You tell what you are by the things you wear, by the spirit in which your burdens bear, by the kind of things at which you laugh, by the records you play on the phonograph. You tell what you are by the way you walk, by the things of which you delight to talk, by the manner in which you bear defeat, by so simple a thing as how you eat. By the books you choose from the well-filled shelf: In these ways and more, you tell on yourself; so there's really no particle of sense, in an effort to keep up a false pretence (The Lighted Pathway).

Day 251

Jesus replied ... Bring them here to me. (Matthew 14:16-18)
Jesus replied ... bring the boy to me. (Matthew 17:17)
Jesus sent ... saying ... bring them to me. (Matthew 21:1,2)

Daily reading: Genesis 24:1-28

Do you ever find yourself saying, 'But, I'm not …'? If ever there was proof that the Lord uses the 'things that are not' (1 Cor.1:27,28), this is it. He used 'despised' barley loaves, not the finest of the wheat; a foolish lad, not a wise intellectual; and the 'weak' ass and colt instead of a mighty steed. What a lovely, unforgettable way He had of teaching His disciples not to be dismissive. Three times they would have sent people away; three times He looked on unlikely instruments and commanded, 'Bring ... to Me.' Three times the word of the King in Matthew's Gospel broadened the narrow view of His subjects!

Bring them to Jesus, sweet praises of love,
Rrising like incense to heaven above;
Let songs of gladness for mercies renewed,
Bear on bright pinions the heart's gratitude.
Bring them to Jesus, our needs by the way,
Asking in weakness for strength as our day,
Bring empty vessels, the fountain o'erflows,
Bringing the briars He gives us the rose.
Bring them to Jesus, the puzzles we meet,
Casting our doubts at His crucified feet,
Wait till the Master Himself shall explain,
Every strange link in life's wonderful chain.
Bring them to Jesus, our gifts tho' but small
His touch of blessing will hallow them all;
As on the hillside the thousands be fed
With the lad's offering of fishes and bread.
Bring them to Jesus in confident prayer,
Longings that others His goodness may share;
Sure of such asking He never can tire,
Since His own Spirit it creates the desire.
(Eliza E. Hewitt)

Day 252

His own blood. (Hebrews 9:12)
His own blood. (Hebrews 13:12)
His own blood. (Acts 20:28)

Daily reading: Genesis 24:29-67

1. The greatest passport: He entered into the holy place by it.
2. The greatest power: He separated a holy people by it.
3. The greatest preciousness: He redeemed lost sinners by it (1 Pet.1:18,19).
4. The greatest price: He obtained churches for His Father by it.
5. The greatest privilege: He opened up the way to worship by it (Heb.10:19).

The volume of blood that was shed in the Old Testament has been surpassed by the value of blood that was shed in the New. Why? Because it was 'HIS OWN.'

What can wash away my sin? Nothing but the blood of Jesus.
What can make me whole again? Nothing but the blood of Jesus.
O precious is the flow that makes me white as snow;
No other fount I know; nothing but the blood of Jesus.
For my pardon this I see: nothing but the blood of Jesus.
For my cleansing this my plea: nothing but the blood of Jesus.
Nothing can for sin atone: nothing but the blood of Jesus.
Naught of good that I have done: nothing but the blood of Jesus.
This is all my hope and peace: nothing but the blood of Jesus.
This is all my righteousness: nothing but the blood of Jesus.
(Robert Lowry)

Day 253

The children of Israel sent a present unto Eglon the king of Moab. But Ehud made him a dagger which had two edges. (Judges 3:15,16 KJV)

Daily reading: Genesis 25

What do you have to use against the Adversary today - a present or a home-made sword? Ehud had no second-hand, hand-me-down, passed-on defence. No, he'd made it his own, a weapon that filled and fitted his hand. Is today's witness so carefully crafted by you that you're comfortable with it? When God says, 'Speak', are you ready to speak? Or are you going to sweet-talk someone with 'a present'? What will you leave them? What sort of impression will you make? To win the person, you need to slay the enemy. To slay the enemy, you need a word from the Lord. Whatever He's helped you to prepare is His, it's yours - and theirs!

Thy word, almighty Lord, where'er it enters in,
Is sharper than a two-edged sword, to slay the man of sin.
Thy word is power and life; it bids confusion cease,
And changes envy, hatred, strife, to love, and joy, and peace.
Then let our hearts obey the gospel's glorious sound;
And all its fruits, from day to day, be in us and abound.
(James Montgomery)

Day 254

My brothers and sisters, believers in our glorious Lord Jesus Christ must not show favoritism. (James 2:1)

If only E. Stanley Jones' great observation could be permanently printed on our minds: 'A new measuring stick has been brought into being. It is not who you are, but Whose.' Our Shepherd hasn't asked us to grade His sheep. Our King hasn't asked us to class His subjects.

> Let me look at the crowd as the Saviour did,
> Till my eyes with tears grow dim;
> Let me look till I pity the wandering sheep
> And love them for love of Him.
> (Author unknown)

Day 255

As she stood behind him at his feet weeping, she began to wet his feet with her tears. Then she wiped them with her hair, kissed them and poured perfume on them. (Luke 7:38)

Daily reading: Genesis 27:1-29

The Lord must have been kissed many times but only two occasions are recorded in the Gospels. What contrasts we see! The first time He was kissed by a woman and the second time by a man (Judas). The first kiss was placed on His feet; Judas no doubt kissed the Lord's cheeks. The first kiss was in daylight and indoors; the second at the darkness of midnight and outdoors. The same Greek word is used both times - it means 'to kiss fervently.' The first kiss betrayed genuine love and devotion; the second was a kiss of treachery and betrayal.

> She kissed His feet - those feet that trod the lonely path below,
> From which the crimson blood so soon would flow - she kissed His feet.
> Thus every one who knows the Saviour's frank, forgiving love,
> And hopes to fall before His feet above, has kissed God's Son.
> Yes, kissed His feet in pledge that they
> Would not through all life's trying way His footsteps shun.
> (William Blane)

Day 256

But if you suffer for doing good and you endure it, this is commendable before God. To this you were called, because Christ suffered for you … (1 Peter 2:20-21)

In what sense is suffering part of the Christian's calling? The background to this verse was the brutal treatment dealt out to Christian household slaves. Its severity might even have reflected the hostility of pagan masters to Christ-like behaviour which showed up their own unreasonable conduct. The display of Christ-like graces in a saved sinner may trouble the conscience of the unsaved around us so much that they inflict all kinds of abuse on us. When this happens to us let's try to remember: " It is enough for students to be like their teachers, and servants like their masters" (Matt.10:25).

Prince of glory condescended, He has favored me;
On the cross He meekly suffered my poor soul to free;
He has cleansed my inner being, changed my life of wrong;
How His touch of healing virtue fills my heart with song.
He was crucified for me, He was crucified for me,
He was crucified for me on the cross of Calvary.
See the Sov'reign of creation, King of earth and skies,
All for sinful man's salvation thus He dies, He dies;
Yet He lives, a mighty Monarch, reigns o'er every foe,
Causing mortal man to triumph over sin below.
(Barney E. Warren)

Day 257

Therefore, as God's chosen people, holy and dearly loved, clothe yourselves with compassion, kindness, humility, gentleness and patience. (Colossians 3:12)

Daily reading: Genesis 28

Let me be a little kinder, let me be a little blinder
To the faults of those about me; let me praise a little more.
Let me be, when I am weary, just a little bit more cheery;
Let me serve a little better those that I am I striving for.
Let me be a little braver, when temptation bids me waver;
Let me strive a little harder to be all that I should be.
Let me be a little meeker with the brother that is weaker;
Let me think more of my neighbor and a little less of me.
(Author unknown)

Day 258

He that is slow to anger is better than the mighty.
(Proverbs 16:32)

Daily reading: Genesis 29

Do minor irritants annoy you? Despite his exemplary behaviour, little David met with elder brother Eliab's accusations (1 Sam.17:28). But David wasn't ruffled by little insults, even from big men. However, when he saw the giant Philistine defying the God of Israel, his godly anger was stirred. When the Lord was insulted, He didn't retaliate, when He suffered He didn't threaten, but when merchants turned His Father's house into a den of thieves, His zealous wrath was seen. You can tell a person's true size by the size of the things that annoy them, can't you?

> Slow to anger, full of kindness, rich in mercy, Lord thou art,
> Wash me in thy healing fountain, take away my sinful heart.
> May thy ever gracious spirit lead me in the way of truth;
> May I learn the voice of wisdom in the early days of youth.
> (Fanny Crosby)

Day 259

In fact, the law requires that nearly everything be cleansed with blood, and without the shedding of blood there is no forgiveness. (Hebrews 9:22)

Daily reading: Genesis 30:1-24

A doctor says that to completely cleanse the hands of bacteria is virtually impossible. The use of turpentine, benzoline, xylol, alcohol or any number of antiseptics, fails to make the hands surgically clean. Even more ineffective was Pilate's hand washing, by which he intended to signify his innocence of moral guilt. But the Lord Jesus, as the unblemished Lamb being led to the slaughter that day, was to give unsoiled hands to be nailed to the cross, and there give His life, shedding His blood for the forgiveness of our sins. That was how we were purged and cleansed, so we can ascend into the hill of the Lord, being completely clean (Jn 13:10) and having "clean hands" (Ps.24:4).

> Lord, through the blood of the Lamb that was slain - cleansing for me;
> From all the guilt of my sins now I claim - cleansing from thee.
> Sinful and dark though the past may have been,
> Many the crushing defeats I have seen,

Yet on thy promise, O Lord, now I lean, cleansing for me.
From all the sins over which I have wept - cleansing for me;
Far, far away by the blood-current swept - cleansing for me.
Jesus, thy promise I dare to believe, and as I come thou wilt surely receive,
That over sin I may never more grieve - cleansing for me.
(Herbert H. Booth)

Day 260

For the Son of Man came to seek and to save the lost.
(Luke 19:10)

Daily reading: Genesis 30:25-43

How does a shepherd find a lost sheep? He goes out searching and he calls and calls. All the time, he's also listening for the cry of the lost sheep. If it doesn't call, it may remain lost. The Good Shepherd, Jesus, came all the way from heaven to look for us, but He's also waiting for us to call out for help. He'll always hear. "Whosoever shall call on the name of the Lord shall be saved" (Acts 2:21). If we don't call, we will be lost.

Jesus is our Shepherd, wiping every tear;
Folded in His bosom, what have we to fear?
Only let us follow whither He doth lead,
To the thirsty desert or the dewy mead.
Jesus is our Shepherd: Well we know His voice;
How its gentlest whisper makes our heart rejoice!
Even when He chideth, tender is its tone;
None but He shall guide us; we are His alone.
(Hugh Stowell)

Day 261

A truthful witness saves lives, but a false witness is deceitful.
(Proverbs 14:25)

Daily reading: Genesis 31:1-21

One night a motorist was run down by a train at a grade crossing. The old signal man in charge of the crossing had to appear in court. After a severe cross-examination, he was still unshaken. He said he'd waved his lantern frantically, but all to no avail. The following day the superintendent of the line called him into his office. "You did wonderfully well yesterday, Tom," he said. "I was afraid at first that you might waver." "No, sir," replied Tom, "but I was afraid the lawyer was going to ask me whether or not my lantern was lit!" We might wonder what the reaction of the superintendent was to Tom's frank admission. Did he congratulate him on his luck or take him to task for his carelessness? Regardless, we can't expect to be effective in warning people of what's coming if our light for God isn't lit and shining brightly – we'll just be going through the motions.

Day 262

Thou hast enlarged me when I was in distress. (Psalm 4:1 KJV)

Daily reading: Genesis 31:22-55

This is one of God's great works in the lives of His own. Instead of being shrivelled by distress, we can actually be enlarged. The trials that cause the greatest confinement, the pressures that bring such a sense of restriction, needn't only emphasise our personal limitations. They can be used, in His miraculous and mysterious ways, to deepen our awareness of Himself, to widen the application of His Word, to heighten our appreciation of His will, and to lengthen daily communion with our God. These are the dimensions of real enlargement!

Day 263

Every word of God is flawless; he is a shield to those who take refuge in him. (Proverbs 30:5)

Daily reading: Genesis 32

'Life-saving Bible for museum,' was the headline in the newspaper. It was the story of how the small New Testament which stopped a bullet from killing a soldier during World War 1, was being donated to the Gordon Highlander's museum. The bullet had penetrated most of the inch-thick bible that was kept in Private Mackie's chest pocket, but his life had been saved. It's good that this small Bible is on display, and perhaps the Spirit of God will challenge someone's heart about its power to save from sin, but in another sense it's all too easy today to consign the Bible to the museum and forget about it. May we treasure the words of His mouth more than our daily bread! (Job 23:12).

The Lord is my Refuge, my Strength, and Shield, and this of a truth I know;
His tender protection is o'er me still, my comfort where'er I go.
The Lord is my Refuge, my Strength, and Shield, all glory to Him I'll give,
And sing of His mercy by night and day, for only in Him I live.
(Fanny Crosby)

Day 264

Cast your cares on the Lord and he will sustain you; he will never let the righteous be shaken. (Psalm 55:22)

Daily reading: Genesis 33

Child of my love, lean hard, and let me feel the pressure of thy care. I know thy burden, child, I shaped it, poised in my own hand, made no proportion in its weight to thy unladed strength. For soon as I laid it on, I said, `I shall be near and when he leans on me, this burden shall be mine, not his.' So shall I keep my child within the circling arms of mine own love. Here lay it down, nor fear to impose it on a shoulder which upholds the government of worlds. Yet closer come - Thou art not near enough. I would embrace thy care, so I might feel my child reposing on my breast. Thou lovest me! I know it! Doubt not then, but - loving me - lean hard (Elizabeth Prentiss).

Day 265

The righteous shall flourish like a palm tree. (Psalm 92:12)

Daily reading: Genesis 34

Hardly anything of the palm tree goes to waste. In addition to its dates, it's a source of sugar and oil, and its leaves provide roofing material. Growing some eighty feet high, and luxuriant in its foliage, it's a striking picture of a godly believer. How does the palm tree survive and flourish in the dry conditions around it? The answer lies in its long root, which drives deep down to the water source. Are you flourishing in your fruit-bearing? It's impossible unless you're continually drawing upon the rich supply of the Word of God. If we'd only live our lives in full obedience to Scripture, there'd be nothing in what we say and do that would go to waste!

Day 266

Indeed I have taken much trouble to prepare for the house of the LORD ... I have prepared ... and you may add to them. (1 Chronicles 22:14)

Daily reading: Genesis 35

No amount of wealth could sufficiently mirror on earth the infinite and eternal glory of heaven. Even when three thousand seven hundred and fifty tons of gold, thirty-seven thousand five hundred tons of silver, plus vast amounts of bronze and iron had been donated by David, he encouraged his son to give what he could. And, without feeling inferior, he did. Do you feel limited? Less able than others? That what you have to offer doesn't amount to much? Listen, if it seems that others have 'taken much trouble to prepare for the house of the LORD', just remember that 'you may add to them.' After all, isn't it often the case that the fewer the words the louder the Amen?

Day 267

… making the most of every opportunity, because the days are evil. (Ephesians 5:16)

Daily reading: Genesis 36

Rebekah was quick to respond to Eleazer's request for a drink. She was equally quick and eager to be of further service to the stranger. She offered to draw water for the camels too. It wasn't a small job; camels don't drink often, but when they do they drink a lot – as much as ten gallons at a draught – and there were ten camels! But "she quickly emptied her jar into the trough, ran back to the well to draw more water, and drew enough for all his camels" (Gen.24:19). No missed opportunities. No job half-done.

Let us not dream of ever looking back,
Let not our knees be feeble, hands be slack,
O make us strong to labour, strong to bear,
From the rising of the morning till the stars appear.
(Author unknown)

Day 268

He must become greater; I must become less." The one who comes from above is above all; the one who is from the earth belongs to the earth, and speaks as one from the earth. The one who comes from heaven is above all. (John 3:30-31)

Daily reading: Genesis 37

Of all the planets in our solar system, Mercury is nearest to the sun. If thirty-seven million miles can be described as "near", Mercury is always 'near' the sun; indeed, so near that in former years it was hardly ever seen. The medieval astronomer Copernicus is reported as saying that he deeply regretted that he had to die without having seen this planet, though he had watched for it with care. Spurgeon observed that as Mercury is usually lost in the rays of the sun, that is where you and I ought to be 'so close to Christ, the Sun of righteousness, that the people who are trying to observe our movements can scarcely see us at all.'

Day 269

"All right, say 'Shibboleth.'" If he said, "Sibboleth," because he could not pronounce the word correctly, they seized him and killed him at the fords of the Jordan ... (Judges 12:6)

Daily reading: Genesis 38

Shibboleth is the Hebrew word for a grain of wheat. Nowadays in English it has come to mean a party slogan or cliche. To soldiers from Ephraim long ago it became the most important word in their lives; failure to pronounce it correctly meant death at the hands of their enemy. Life or death from a grain of wheat. Christians confidently assert the lasting truth of Christ's words about a grain of wheat dying in order to bring life; they know He was describing His own death for them, and the sacrificial lifestyle of His would-be followers. That's not an outdated cliche; it's **the** life or death question. Of course, as Peter found, it's one thing to say we're committed, and another thing to live it.

Day 270

And Moses said to the people, 'Do not be afraid. Stand still, and see the salvation of the LORD, which He will accomplish for you today.' (Exodus 14:13)

Daily reading: Genesis 39

With the tyrannical taskmasters in hot pursuit and the impassable waters of the Red Sea ahead, how could Israel 'Stand still'? Because God had said it. With the prospect of such drastic upheaval, how could the psalmist, 'Be still'? Because the Lord of hosts had said it. In dying weakness, Wesley summoned his energy to cry out, 'The best of all is, God is with us.' If we feel fearful, trapped, overwhelmed, we can know the stillness because God speaks it, gives it and delivers it personally.

> Be still, my soul, thy God doth undertake.
> To guide the future as He hath the past.
> Thy hope, thy confidence let nothing shake;
> All now mysterious shall be bright at last"
> (Katherine von Schlegel).

<u>**Day 271**</u>

Do nothing out of selfish ambition or vain conceit. Rather, in humility value others above yourselves. (Philippians 2:3) So whatever you wish that others would do to you, do also to them, for this is the Law and the Prophets. (Matthew 7:2)

Daily reading: Genesis 40

I do not mind my P's and Q's, how careless I must B;
Nor do my actions always suit my Neighbors to a T.
I think perhaps the greatest fault that I can now recall—
I make my I's a lot too large, and all my U's too small.
(Reginald Holmes)

<u>**Day 272**</u>

Therefore, if anyone is in Christ, the new creation has come: The old has gone, the new is here! (2 Corinthians 5:17)

Daily reading: Genesis 41:1-28

Sometimes, we think too small and tell ourselves, "I can never change." One preacher said, "We presume too much and believe too little. In Jesus Christ, God renders all our final conclusions premature ... opens closed doors, brings resurrection, reveals possibilities, reclaims the lost, liberates the cursed and possessed, and changed the unchangeable." Are you struggling with part of the old nature, or a habit that won't die away? Don't conclude, "I can't help it, it's just the way I'm made." Think of what God has made you, and set about the business of working out what He has worked in.

Attend, while God's exalted Son doth his own glories show:
"Behold, I sit upon my throne, creating all things new.
"Nature and sin are passed away, and the old Adam dies;
My hands a new foundation lay, see the new world arise.
"I'll be a Sun of Righteousness to the new heav'ns I make;
None but the new-born heirs of grace my glories shall partake."
Mighty Redeemer! set me free from my old state of sin;
O make my soul alive to thee, create new powers within.
Renew mine eyes, and form mine ears, and mold my heart afresh;
Give me new passions, joys, and fears, and turn the stone to flesh.
Far from the regions of the dead, from sin, and earth, and hell,
In the new world that grace has made, I would for ever dwell.
(Isaac Watts)

Day 273

Mary took a pound of very costly oil of spikenard. (John 12:3 NKJV)
Nicodemus brought a mixture of myrrh and aloes, about seventy-five pounds. (John 19:39)

Daily reading: Genesis 41:29-57

Mary brought a pound of ointment to anoint the Lord's feet whilst Nicodemus brought seventy-five times that to anoint His whole body, when typically only five pounds of spices were used for a burial. It was the Saviour of sinners that moved both of them to offer Him something that emitted a fragrance before and after Calvary. What we bring today in our worship will not be valued in weight but in how much fragrance of Him that we place into the hands of our High Priest.

Day 274

But to stop this thing from spreading any further among the people, we must warn them to speak no longer to anyone in this name. (Acts 4:17)

Daily reading: Genesis 42

There's a real challenge in the truth of these words, for if we keep quiet the Gospel won't spread. That was the objective of the rulers and the elders, but Peter raised an objection: God has commanded us to speak, and you forbid us to speak. "We ought to obey God rather than men" (Acts 5:29). Thank God for those faithful men, and men and women like them, who have dared to speak out in obedience to the command to go, make, baptize, teach (Matt.28:19,20). Speak out and live out the Gospel today, so that in defiance of opposition it will spread further among the people.

Spread the good news of salvation, News, oh so wondrously sweet,
Unto the perishing round you gladly the story repeat.
Spread the good news of salvation; many, perchance, have not heard,
Blessed salvation is promised, only believe in his word. [Chorus]
Spread the good news of salvation, loudly the message proclaim;
Tell unto all that he offers pardon thro' Jesus dear name.
(Ella E. Miles)

Day 275

Command those who are rich in this present world not to be arrogant nor to put their hope in wealth, which is so uncertain, but to put their hope in God, who richly provides us with everything for our enjoyment. (1 Timothy 6:17)
Those who trust in their riches will fall, but the righteous will thrive like a green leaf. (Proverbs 11:28)

Daily reading: Genesis 43

Rudyard Kipling once advised a group of students not to make money, power or fame their goals for, one day, they would meet a Man who did not care for any of these things. "Then," said Kipling, "you will know how poor you are." This world is passing away and we shall soon meet the Man who, for our sakes, became poor, that we through His poverty might become rich in a way that the world knows nothing of. What is your aim today, to please yourself in the transient things of time, or to please Him?

Trust not in man, the arm of flesh will fail;
Trust not in man, his strength cannot avail;
Trust not in man, though great may be his boast;
Trusts not in man - who trusts in him is lost.
Trust thou in God, in secret to Him pray,
Trust thou in God, He'll be your strength and stay;
Trust thou in God, make Him thy dearest friend.
Trust Thou in God, He'll keep thee to the end.
(J. Robertson)

Day 276

Consider your ways! (Haggai 1:7 NKJV)
Consider what I say. (2 Timothy 2:7 NKJV)
Consider the Apostle and High Priest. (Hebrews 3:1 NKJV)

Daily reading: Genesis 44

The word 'consider' can mean understanding with the heart as well as the intellect; it can also mean to discover, which involves search and concentration; it can also imply to fully observe – in fact the English word comes from the Latin word for star. How often we gaze up intently at night and see more and more the longer we 'consider' the heavens. Let's analyze our ways as the Lord exhorts through Haggai and get them in perspective, as Paul encourages. In other words, don't let things drift. Bring things into focus by concentrating on the Lord in God's presence on our behalf. When we truly consider, we'll discover the link between the earthly and the heavenly.

O Mighty God! When I thy works consider
Which thou hast formed by thine all-wise command;
And see the care thou to thy works dost render,
That all who live may feed from out thy hand:
In songs of praise my heart bursts forth to sing:
O mighty God! O mighty God!
In songs of praise my heart bursts forth to sing:
O mighty God! O mighty God!
(Carl Gustav Boberg)

Day 277

With him will I speak mouth to mouth. (Numbers 12:8 KJV) ... you, Lord, have been seen face to face. (Numbers 14:14) For they shall see eye to eye. (Isaiah 52:8 NKJV)

Daily reading: Genesis 45

How well those three phrases describe the nearness of God, and of nearness to God. Could anything be closer? Yes, because they all refer to experiencing Him on earth. But it will be 'very far better' to be near Him in heaven! As President McKinley of the U.S.A. was dying, having been shot, he whispered, 'Nearer, my God, to Thee ... Nearer, my God, to Thee.'

When our earthly days are ended, we shall (present nearness past)
Be mouth to mouth and face to face: eye to eye with Him at last.
(Author unknown)

Day 278

What good is it, my brothers and sisters, if someone claims to have faith but has no deeds? Can such faith save them? (James 2:14)

Daily reading: Genesis 46

You may bring to your office, and put in a frame, a motto as fine as its paint, but if you're a crook when you're playing the game, that motto won't make you a saint. You can stick up the placards all over the wall, but here is the word I announce: It is not the motto that hangs on the wall, but the motto you live that counts. If the motto says, "Smile," and you carry a frown; "Do it now," and you linger and wait; if the motto says "Help," and you trample men down; if the motto says "Love," and you hate—you won't get away with the mottoes you install, for truth will come forth with a bounce. It is not the motto that hangs on the wall, but the motto you live, that counts (Kalends).

Day 279

... Joshua the son of Nun, Moses' assistant, one of his choice men. (Numbers 11:28 NKJV)

Daily reading: Genesis 47

After receiving God's unchangeable statement about his life's end, Moses' absolute priority was for God to choose a successor. Joshua mightn't have desired the task, but he was prepared for it. He'd done battle to defend the people of God; He'd known the Spirit of God working with him; He'd experienced the unique privilege of accompanying Moses to a place of special nearness to God. He'd built up a righteous love for the holiness of God. Now the Jordan awaited, and it would be Joshua, not Moses, who must provide the lead. A choice man indeed. Good men and women have done their part. Are you ready to take over? How well prepared are you to take up where they leave off?

> Ready to suffer grief or pain, ready to stand the test;
> Ready to stay at home and send others if He sees best.
> Ready to go, ready to stay, ready my place to fill;
> Ready for service lowly or great, ready to do His will.
> Ready to go, ready to bear, ready to watch and pray;
> Ready to stand aside and give till He shall clear the way.
> Ready to speak, ready to think, ready with heart and mind;
> Ready to stand where He sees fit, ready His will to find.
> (A.C. Palmer)

Day 280

... where our forerunner, Jesus, has entered on our behalf. (Hebrews 6:20)

Daily reading: Genesis 48

In all the Lord's activity as Man on earth, we read that He lay, knelt, sat, stood and walked - but we never read that He ran. Before He came, other men were famous for their running: Asahel was killed by being a good runner (2 Sam.2:23), Ahimaaz ran, but had nothing to say when he got there (2 Sam.18:29), and David ran in the certainty of being victorious (1 Sam.17:48). Our Saviour never ran. He went at a dignified pace: no one had to run to catch up with Him. He went on to the cross, never running to it or away from it. Men thought it was the end, but it was only the starting-blocks for the Forerunner on His way back into God's presence - running ahead for us to be our High Priest.

Day 281

If God be for us, who can be against us? (Romans 8:31)

Daily reading: Genesis 49

Paul had plenty opposition to contend with, and so do we. The world around us disregards our Saviour, discourages our work and disparages our faith. Satan tempts to sin and despair. But what Paul's really asking here is: "Who can be against us effectively?" The answer is no-one! God is greater than all our foes and with His power behind us, His presence with us and His path ahead of us, no opposition can prevail. We only have to trust Him and ask for His help.

Jehovah is our Strength, and He shall be our Song
We shall o'ercome at length although our foes be strong.
In vain does Satan then oppose, for God is stronger than His foes.
(William Henry Havergal)

Day 282

Therefore I do not run like someone running aimlessly; I do not fight like a boxer beating the air. (1 Corinthians 9:26)

Daily reading: Genesis 50

A young boy dreamed of becoming the fastest runner in the world. His coach told him, "It's great to have a dream, but to attain your dream you must build a ladder to it. Here is the ladder to your dream. The first rung is determination, the second rung is dedication, the third rung is discipline, and the fourth is attitude." The result of all that motivation was that Jesse Owens went on to win four gold medals in the 1936 Berlin Olympics. Christian, are you 'going for gold'? Check out your determination, dedication, disciple and attitude, and run. Run in such a way as to get the prize - stretching forward!

Take my life and let it be consecrated, Lord, to thee.
Take my moments and my days; let them flow in ceaseless praise,
Take my hands and let them move at the impulse of thy love.
Take my feet and let them be swift and beautiful for thee.
(Frances Ridley Havergal)

Day 283

He also made the stars. (Genesis 1:16)

Daily reading: Luke 1:1-40

If God had to describe how He made the stars, the Bible would be a very large book. It isn't, however, a book on astronomy. God limits His description of the starry heavens to just two words in the Hebrew Bible: 'stars too.' Even the Hebrew word for star is quite obscure and seems to be connected with 'blazing.' Yet astronomers have spent their lives probing into the mysteries of the heavenly bodies. Their Creator walked this earth, for He had created and placed us on it. The stars mean little to Him, but He suffered and died for us. If even the stars are exhorted to praise Him (Ps.148:3), then so should we!

He made the sun that day by day pours down its radiance bright.
He made yon stately moon that rules in silvery pomp the night.
But all those tiny twinkling specks as far as eye can go,
I watch with wonder when I think, 'He made the stars also.'
(Author unknown)

Day 284

The Philistines took him and put out his eyes, and ... said: 'Our god has delivered into our hands Samson our enemy!' ... So they called for Samson from the prison. (Judges 16:21- 25)

Daily reading: Luke 1:41-80

Samson's name means sunlight, but he'd darkened the skies of his life many times by his carelessness and now the sun was eclipsed. Samson's wandering eyes had been his trouble (Judg.14:1; 16:1). He was famous for his physical strength, but if only he'd been as strong as Job, 'I have made a covenant with my eyes; why then should I look upon a young woman?' (Job 31:1) or heeded the Lord's advice in Matthew 18:9, 'And if your eye causes you to sin, pluck it out and cast it from you.' Instead, the Philistines seized him and gouged out his eyes. Picture him at the end, a sightless shambling shadow of his former self being led by the hand to the palace of Dagon. Temptation seldom breaks down your front door; it quietly and cunningly enters the open door of your mind.

> Lord, who throughout those forty days for us did fast and pray,
> Teach us with you to mourn our sins and close by you to stay.
> As you with Satan did contend and did the vict'ry win,
> O give us strength in you to fight, in you to conquer sin.
> As you did hunger bear and thirst, so teach us, gracious Lord,
> To die to self and always live by your most holy word.
> (Claudia Frances Hernaman)

Day 285

This same Jesus ... will come back in the same way you have seen him go into heaven. (Acts 1:11)

Daily reading: Luke 2

> That same Jesus Who, ascending, passed through Heaven's portals wide,
> Soon will come, from Heaven descending, to receive His blood-bought bride.
> Yes! Himself, and not another, we shall see His form most fair,
> And, His own caught up together, we shall meet Him in the air.
> But while here, by foes surrounded, think that He Himself was tried:
> He has all our foes confounded; He Himself is by our side.
> As our Shepherd, forth He leads us, our High Priest, for us He pleads,
> For the conflict fits and feeds us, and Himself, our Captain, leads.
> (Author unknown)

Day 286

Daniel ... knelt down ... three times that day, and prayed and gave thanks before his God, as was his custom. (Daniel 6:10)

Daily reading: Luke 3

One night a British soldier was discovered creeping back to his quarters. Suspicious, his commanding officers immediately charged him with communicating with the enemy. He pleaded innocent, insisting that he'd been out to find solitude in which to pray. Asked if he made a habit of it, he said that he did. 'Then get down and pray!' roared the officer. 'You've never needed it as much as you do now.' Expecting the death penalty, the young man poured out his heart in prayer to God in the power of the Holy Spirit. 'You may go,' declared the officer. 'If you hadn't drilled so often, you couldn't have done so well at review. I believe your story.' 'I am a man of prayer,' said David (Ps.109:4). Are you? It will show if you are.

Almighty God, in humble prayer, to Thee our souls we lift,
Do Thou our waiting minds prepare for Thy most needful gift.
We ask not golden streams of wealth along our path to flow;
We ask not undecaying health, nor length of years below.
We ask not honors, which an hour may bring and take away;
We ask not pleasure, pomp and power, lest we should go astray.
We ask for wisdom—Lord, impart the knowledge how to live;
A wise and understanding heart to all before Thee give.
(James Montgomery)

Day 287

"Now arise, Lord God, and come to your resting place, you and the ark of your might. May your priests, Lord God, be clothed with salvation, may your faithful people rejoice in your goodness. (2 Chronicles 6:41)

Daily reading: Luke 4

Christ described Himself as "the Master of the house" (Matt.10.25); the writer to the Hebrews calls Him "Son over God's house" (Heb.3:6). The Master is one who has absolute authority and the strength to exert it. The temple that Solomon built would have been an empty shell without the Ark. It was more than a piece of furniture; in God's eyes its form and substance depicted Christ as the One who is mighty in mercy. Now the heavenly temple is filled with the glory of the presence of our mighty Redeemer. Rejoice, all you who are clothed with His salvation!

Lord, Thy glory fills the heaven;
Earth is with its fullness stored;
Unto Thee be glory given,
Holy, holy, holy Lord.
Thus Thy glorious Name confessing,
We adopt the angels' cry,
Holy, holy, holy blessing
Thee, the Lord our God most high.
(Richard Mant)

Day 288

Be shepherds of God's flock that is under your care, watching over them—not because you must, but because you are willing, as God wants you to be. (1 Peter 5:2)

Daily reading: Luke 5

How valuable are the times when a lot of personal candidness results from a little pastoral care. So many are hurting, but a smile often conceals in the church what the tear reveals in the chair. There's a whole ministry for the shepherd-hearted waiting to be fulfilled at the fireside, isn't there? It's where we can kneel with our brothers and sisters, helping them to lean trustingly upon the Lord. How much we need to share the burden of those who would love to come up out of the wilderness, leaning upon their Beloved (Song of Solomon 8:5). Will He use us to bring them within reach?

> Would you be a sunbeam filled with Heaven's light,
> Shedding forth its beauty over scenes of night?
> In this world of sorrow, sickness, sin and woe,
> Try to be a blessing everywhere you go.
> Where the tears are falling and the hearts are sad,
> Take some Gospel message that will make them glad;
> Strive to give them comfort by some loving deed,
> Try to be a blessing in the time of need.
> Be a blessing on life's weary mile,
> Be a blessing with a word or smile;
> Be a blessing, everywhere the same;
> Try to be a blessing in the Master's name.
> (Johnson Oatman Jnr.)

Day 289

Never be lacking in zeal, but keep your spiritual fervor, serving the Lord. (Romans 12:11)

Daily reading: Luke 6

'Live so as to be missed!' was the advice of godly Robert Murray McCheyne. He obviously lived that out because over 6,000 people attended in his funeral in 1843 – he was just 29. Paul lived it out, too. What a vacuum was left after his departure! No more letters of encouragement, no more instruction and no more counsel from his pen. What a loss to the people of God! How the saints would reminisce over the things he'd said and done in his own inimitable way!

How the disciples would have missed the Lord after His ascension. Of course, he knew that and so he promised them He'd send them another Comforter. If we're not purposefully living to be missed, aren't we missing the purpose of living?

Day 290

At that time Joshua went and destroyed the Anakites ... from all the hill country of Israel. No Anakites were left in Israelite territory ... (Joshua 11:21,22)

Daily reading: Luke 7

Joshua waged war on the gigantic Anakim until there was none left in the land. And there should be none in our lives either. If there's a big issue in our life, we must ask the Lord to identify it and grant us the Spirit-given power to defeat it, no matter how gigantic it might seem. 'You ... are from God,' and can 'overcome ... because He who is in you is greater than he who is in the world' (1 Jn 4:4). The name 'Anakim' means a necklace, a choker, and carries the thought of strangling. Beware of the apparently attractive things of life that can so often develop from a toehold to a foothold, to a stronghold, and finally to a stranglehold!

He all my grief has taken and all my sorrows borne,
In temptation He's my strong and mighty tow'r;
I have all for Him forsaken and all my idols torn
From my heart, and now He keeps me by His pow'r.
Though all the world forsake me and Satan tempt me sore,
Through Jesus I shall safely reach the goal;
He's the Lily of the Valley, the Bright and Morning Star,
He's the greatest of ten thousand to my soul.
(Charles W. Fry)

Day 291

That power is the same as the mighty strength he exerted when he raised Christ from the dead. (Ephesians 1:19-20)

Daily reading: Luke 8

When you think about it, isn't it a bit absurd that we still measure the power of racing car engines in terms of horsepower? New terms have had to be invented to measure computing power because we don't yet understand enough about ourselves to measure it in terms of quantified brain-power.

Man's power isn't in his muscles, but in his ability to engineer, to make machines stronger than himself to do his will. Yet all this can only be contrasted rather than compared to God's power. How was divine power mightily displayed? Not in lifeless engineering, but in resurrection - and God promises to empower us with this immeasurable force in our Christian service!

Day 292

Now to you who believe, this stone is precious.
(1 Peter 2:17)

Daily reading: Luke 9

I'd rather have Jesus than silver or gold;
I'd rather have Jesus than have riches untold;
I'd rather have Jesus than houses or land;
I'd rather be led by His nail-pierced hand:
I'd rather have Jesus than men's applause;
I'd rather be faithful to His dear cause;
I'd rather have Jesus than worldwide fame;
I'd rather be true to His holy Name:
Than to be the king of a vast domain
And be held in sin's dread sway.
I'd rather have Jesus than anything
This world affords today.
(Rhea F. Miller)

Day 293

Should your fellow Israelites go to war while you sit here?
(Numbers 32:6)

Daily reading: Luke 10

The fast-flowing Jordan lay ahead and beyond it were Israel's hostile enemies. In Moses' last days among the Israelites he feared for their future. Some of them found the pleasant lands before the Jordan ideal for their agricultural pursuits. Would they lose heart to cross the Jordan and fight at God's command? Moses wouldn't have forgotten the failings of the last generation. They'd refused to proceed into the Promised Land, because they were afraid. What about this generation? Would they follow Joshua into battle, despite their affluence? Perhaps we need to hear these words too. To the credit of the men in Joshua's day, they left their flocks and herds and went on to victory.

Others are ready to give their all in following the Lord Jesus. Are you going or
are you sitting?

My Captain sounds the alarm of war – Awake! the powers of hell are near!
"To arms, to arms!" I hear him cry; "'Tis yours to conquer, or to die!"
Roused by the animating sound, I cast my eager eyes around;
Make haste to gird my armour on, and bid each trembling fear begone.
Hope is my helmet; Christ my shield;
Thy Word, my God, the sword I wield;
With sacred truth my loins are girt, and holy zeal inspires my heart.
Thus armed, I venture on the fight, resolved to put my foes to flight;
While Jesus kindly deigns to spread His conquering banner o'er my head.
(Samuel Stennett)

Day 294

The Lord Jesus, on the night he was betrayed, took bread …
(1 Corinthians 11:23)

Daily reading: Luke 11

Many things happened that night, so why is this singled out? Judas had
bargained and made a covenant with the Scribes and Pharisees about how
much he'd get for betraying Christ. The word betray literally means 'to give
from close beside' and that proximity is what makes his actions so chilling.
Now he was fulfilling that covenant at the same time that the Lord was in the
upper room making a covenant with His disciples; but there was no bargaining
here - it was all about how much He was prepared to give. What a contrast
between thirty pieces of silver on the one hand, and the precious blood of
Christ on the other, which he'd give from close beside a thief who later that day
would be close beside Him in Paradise.

Oh Judas! How couldst thou betray the Lord
Who gave thee life and breath;
And see the Saviour fall a prey to suffering,
Shame, reproach and death!
The solemn vows are now forgot, and sacred friendship all abused;
But Christ foreknew the treacherous plot, nor the deceitful kiss refused. How
could the wretch unmoved survey, a face so lovely and divine;   How such a
friend of friends betray, whose acts to him were all benign!
(Benjamin Beddome)

Day 295

That I may be encouraged together with you by the mutual faith both of you and me. (Romans 1:12 NKJV)

Daily reading: Luke 12

It was gracious of the apostle to put it that way. His long life of affliction and suffering had served to strengthen his faith, so that it must have appeared very robust compared with the faith of some of the disciples in Rome. But even their weak faith brought him comfort. He says so, 'comforted ... each of us by the other's faith ... yours and mine' (RV). So be encouraged - even your faint faith may cheer someone on their way today.

> The slightest breeze that ever blew, some slender grass has wavered;
> The simplest life I ever knew, some other life has flavoured.
> We cannot live our lives alone, for other lives we touch
> Are either strengthened by our own or weakened just as much.
> (Ella Wheeler Wilcox)

Day 296

Add to your faith ... patience. (2 Peter 1:5,6 KJV)
Be patient ... until the Lord's coming. (James 5:7)

Daily reading: Luke 13

John Wesley's godly mother was once complimented by her husband: 'I wonder at your patience that you can tell that blockhead John the same thing twenty times over.' She replied, 'If I had been content to repeat only nineteen times, I would have wasted all my labour.' Something worthwhile must have sunk into the blockhead's brain as he was later to write, "Do all the good you can, by all the means you can, in all the ways you can, in all the places you can, at all the times you can, to all the people you can, as long as ever you can"! Patience is defined as remaining under the trial, having fortitude, perseverance, sufferance, continuance. There is no time limit. James, the practical apostle, encourages us to be patient until the Lord returns! While we're waiting, let's add virtue, knowledge and patience to our faith.

> Patience! O what a grace divine! Giv'n by the God of love and pow'r,
> That leans upon a father's hand, in ev'ry dark, afflicting hour.
> By patience we serenely bear the troubles of our mortal state;
> And wait contented our discharge, nor think our glory comes too late.

Though we in full sensation feel the weight, the wounds our God ordains,
We smile amid our heaviest woes, and triumph in our sharpest pains.
O for this grace to aid us on, and arm with fortitude the breast,
Till life's tumultuous voyage is o'er, we reach the shores of endless rest!
Faith into vision shall resign, hope shall in full fruition die;
And patience in possession end in the bright worlds of bliss on high.
(Thomas Gibbons)

Day 297

**When Jesus had finished saying these things, the crowds were amazed at his teaching, because he taught as one who had authority, and not as their teachers of the law.
(Matthew 7:28,29)**

Daily reading: Luke 14

No-one ever spoke like Christ did, because His words came with authority and the result in this case was amazement. The meaning of the Greek word used indicates that the crowd's jaws were dropping, and they were left not just speechless but dumbfounded. They were gripped by His teaching, but sadly for many of them their recognition of His authority didn't result in a following faith. In the very next chapter, it's Jesus turn to be amazed, although it's a different Greek word used that involves admiration. It was left to a Roman centurion to demonstrate his faith in the authority of the Lord to heal, even from a distance. What are you making of his authority to teach, to heal and even to forgive sins?

At the name of Jesus ev'ry knee shall bow,
Ev'ry tongue confess him King of glory now;
'Tis the Father's pleasure we should call him Lord,
Who from the beginning was the mighty Word.
In your hearts enthrone him; there let him subdue
All that is not holy, all that is not true;
Crown him as your captain in temptation's hour;
Let his will enfold you in its light and pow'r.
(Caroline M. Noel)

Day 298

... those who have believed in God should be careful to maintain good works. These things are good and profitable to men. (Titus 3:8 NKJV)

Good deeds aren't optional, they're obligatory for the Christian, but they must be done in a quiet, unostentatious way that brings glory to God, not to the doer (Matt.5:16). In Ruth's day, it was the reapers who'd done the back-breaking bending to cut and gather the barley and who were required by their master, Boaz, to drop handfuls for the Moabitess to gather. Yet, when Naomi asked her, 'Where have you gleaned today?', she answered, 'The man's name ... was Boaz' (Ruth 2:19). The reapers didn't even get a mention! It was their privilege to glorify their master. 'Your good works' are, after all, those your Lord planned and gave you the opportunity and the ability to do in the first place – so it's right that they should glorify your Father.

Day 299

**Satisfy us in the morning with your unfailing love,
that we may sing for joy and be glad all our days. (Psalm
90:14)**

Daily reading: Luke 16

We watched the dawning of the day,
And as it came I heard Him say,
"This is the day the Lord hath made";
And with these words a golden ray
Of sunshine full of hope, and bright and clear
Shone through the sorrows of the night, and near
To Him, I knew that both this day,
And I myself, were very dear.
(Frances Ridley Havergal)

Day 300

**The tempter ... said, ... 'All these things I will give.'
(Matthew 4:3,9)
Do not lose those things we worked for. (2 John v.8)
We must all appear before the judgement seat.
(2 Corinthians 5:10)**

Daily reading: Luke 17

Is it possible that Satan is making you the same offers that he made to your Master? Is he dangling before you today the incentives of wealth, glamour, opportunities, power and influence? Just imagine the heights to which Paul could have reached! He moved in the right circles and he knew the right people. But after his conversion he counted worldly influence as a load of rubbish! When the Master comes and we stand before the 'Bema' (the judgement-seat) will our hands hold hay, wood or stubble or the things that will stand the test of heaven's fire?

He sits exalted on the throne,
To us as mighty Saviour known,
Our one and only Lord,
He waits with keen, expectant gaze
The coming of that day of days,
The day of His reward.
Before the holy judgement throne
We'll see as we in awe bow down,
Our works in fire be tried.
In view of that devouring flame,
Be this our prayer, this our aim -
"In Him may we abide."
(Charles Mann Luxmoore)

Day 301

"Is it nothing to you, all you who pass by? Look around and see. Is any suffering like my suffering that was inflicted on me, that the Lord brought on me in the day of his fierce anger? (Lamentations 1:12)

Daily reading: Luke 18

At least fourteen different words are chosen prophetically by Isaiah to describe Messiah's experience at the hands of His people and at the hands of His God. His love, through it all, is thus expressed: "Surely He hath borne our griefs, and carried our sorrows." Yes, until His final cry: "It is finished." He knew despising, rejection, grief, sorrows, disesteem, woundings, bruisings, chastisement, lashings, oppression, affliction, travail, sinbearing, and being reckoned a transgressor. For Israel? Yes, and for you and me.

How deep and grievous was the woe
Of Christ upon the cross!
It laid the mighty Saviour low
When hanging there for us.
To bring us pain, He bore the pain
And suffered shame and loss.
(Charles Mann Luxmoore)

Day 302

... offer every part of yourself to him as an instrument of righteousness. (Romans 6:13)

Daily reading: Luke 19

During the Second World War many church buildings in Germany were destroyed. Afterwards, in one town the inhabitants set to work on the restoration of a church building where a statue of Christ lay in pieces. Carefully, the statue was repaired until the arms were stretched out as before. However, the hands were missing - they couldn't be found anywhere. One day there appeared an anonymous sign underneath the statue. It read: 'I have no other hands than your hands'!

> Christ has no hands but our hands to do His work today,
> He has no feet but our feet to lead men in His way,
> He has no tongue but our tongues to tell men how He died,
> He has no help but our help to bring them to His side.
> (Annie Johnson Flint)

Day 303

Do you believe that I am able to do this? (Matthew 9:28)

Daily reading: Luke 20

If Jesus had said, 'Do you believe that I am?', it would have been a question about His identity. However, He asked, 'Do you believe that I am able to do this?', and that was a question about His ability. When two blind men replied, 'Yes, Lord', it was the answer of certainty. They had no doubt at all about who He is or about what He is able to do. His deity and ability were beyond question. Even unsighted men can be united in what they can see by faith. Being united in physical darkness didn't hinder them from being united in spiritual light. Do you also believe, or are you still in the dark?

> Faith is believing, the promise is true,
> Trusting in Jesus your strength to renew;
> Resting so sweetly, secure on His word,
> Shielded from danger with Jesus the Lord.
> Faith is believing, simply receiving,
> What in His promise God has revealed;
> Trust Him forever, doubt Him, no, never,

Till thy petition His Spirit hath sealed.
Faith is believing, the soul's happy rest,
Faith is believing, though sorely oppressed;
Singing in triumph whatever assail,
High on the mountains or low in the vale.
Faith is believing, then doubt Him no more,
Sell all your sorrows, your troubles give o'er;
Soar in the sunlight above every cloud,
Triumph forever, believing in God.
(Daniel Otis Teasley)

Day 304

Then Ishbi-Benob, who was one of the sons of the giant ... thought he could kill David. But Abishai ... came to his aid and struck the Philistine and killed him. (2 Samuel 21:16,17)

Daily reading: Luke 21

David and his men were faced with the familiar problem of giants and dealt with decisive action. Ishbi-Benob means 'a settled life of self, a life of ease.' The enemy's intent is clear - to lull us into satisfaction with a life of self-content. 'Ishbi-Benob ... thought he could kill David. But Abishai ... killed him.' Abishai's name means 'gift of God' and his aid was certainly a welcome gift to David. Selfishness will kill us if we don't kill it by the Spirit's power, which is God's gift to us. Don't veer to the left and don't swing to the right, but don't be self-centred either!

Emptied of self, with holy love filled,
Let ev'ry voice within me be stilled,
Until I hear Thy whispers to me,
Dead to the world but living for Thee.
Human I am and ever will be,
Clothe me with gracious humility;
Purge me from sin and make my heart clean,
Until Thy image in me is seen.
All that I have is laid at Thy feet,
My consecration now is complete;
I would be guided by Thee alone,
Take Thou my heart and make it Thy throne.
(Haldor Lillenas)

Day 305

Pray for your servants to the LORD your God ... for we have added to all our sins the evil of asking a king for ourselves. (1 Samuel 12:19)

Daily reading: Luke 22

Sometimes, wanting to be like others is a much easier option than wanting to be different. Being able to say 'I have what you have' or 'I do what you do' can seem so attractive. But how does God feel about it? For the people in Samuel's day, there was nothing particularly wrong in wanting a king. What was wrong was that they wanted a king more than they wanted God. And today we are up against the same problem: being more worldly will never make us more godly. As Christians, we have enough trouble from the devil without rejecting God's plans for us. Spiritual foresight is always better than saying with hindsight, 'we have added to all our sins.'

Day 306

Whom have I in heaven but you? And earth has nothing I desire besides you. (Psalm 73:25)

Daily reading: Luke 23

Christ for sickness, Christ for health, Christ for poverty, Christ for wealth, Christ for joy, Christ for sorrow, Christ today and Christ tomorrow; Christ my Life, and Christ my Light, Christ for morning, noon and night, Christ when all around gives way, Christ my everlasting Stay; Christ my Rest, and Christ my Food, Christ above my highest good, Christ my Well-beloved Friend, Christ my Pleasure without end; Christ my Saviour, Christ my Lord, Christ my Portion, Christ my God, Christ my Shepherd, I His sheep, Christ Himself my soul to keep (Author unknown).

Day 307

Give me understanding, and I shall live. (Psalm 119:44)
Give me understanding according to Your word.
(Psalm 119:169)
Give me understanding and I shall keep Your law.
(Psalm 119:34)

Our prayer lives can remain private, but the psalmist discloses his inner desire. 'Give me understanding', he cries five times. He longs for discernment, for skill, for prudence; the ability to deal wisely with others. To be a better, wiser, more skilful Christian, in our words. We also long to please the Master better; to speak right words at the right time; to encourage, counsel, and seek to lead others to Christ. Perhaps 'give me' should be our prayer priority, plus the desire to 'give me understanding according to Your word.'

Day 308

They are to remove the ashes from the bronze altar and spread a purple cloth over it. (Numbers 4:13)

Daily reading: Leviticus 1

A purple cloth, with its delightful blend of blue and scarlet, was a fitting way to announce a finished work. With the sacrifice received, the flame extinguished and the ashes removed, God was ready to indicate by this kingly-coloured cloth His approval of all that pointed to the true kingliness and dignity of His majestic Son. Who is the King of glory? He is 'the LORD', the lovely Son of God from heaven; 'mighty in battle', the lowly sufferer of Calvary: the blue of heaven and the scarlet of suffering wonderfully combined. God has spread His own 'purple cloth' over the cross that we might consider not only the sufferings of Christ, but the glories that should follow.

Done is the work that saves!
Once and for ever done.
Finished the righteousness
That clothes th'unrighteous one.
The love that blesses us below
Is flowing freely to us now.
(Horatius Bonar)

Day 309

**Then, leaving her water jar, the woman went back to the town and said to the people, "Come, see a man who told me everything I ever did. Could this be the Messiah?"
(John 4:28,29)**

Why did she leave her waterpot? It was very important to her. She needed water in order to live, and the waterpot in which to carry her water. So, why risk leaving it? Perhaps, for two reasons. First, the wonder of the revelation she'd received overshadowed the importance of the waterpot, and second, perhaps because she knew she'd be coming back again because she wanted further dealings with the Messiah. Her material needs had a place, an important place, but now she'd found the promised One, whose presence and teachings were far more important. She was putting things in their right perspective. Do we?

The world all about me has now no allure:
Its pleasure ring pain, its wisdom is vain;
I seek a foundation that's steadfast and sure:
I'll put Jesus first in my life.
In all that I say, in all that I do,
Throughout the world of toil and strife,
By day and by night, through trust in His might,
I'll put Jesus first in my life.
(James D. Murch)

Day 310

They devoted themselves ... to prayer. (Acts 2:42)
Be joyful in hope, patient in affliction, faithful in prayer.
(Romans 12:12)
Devote yourselves to prayer, being watchful and thankful.
(Colossians 4:2)

Daily reading: Leviticus 3

Is your church prayer meeting a duty or a joy? D.L. Moody said, 'I am so tired of the nuisance of that word 'duty.' A man gets up in a prayer meeting and says he has not much to say - people find it out before he talks two minutes - but he feels it his 'duty' to say something for the Lord and help fill up time. What a nuisance!'

Lord, teach me what I need, and teach me how to pray;
Nor let me ask Thee for Thy grace, not feeling what I say.
(Author unknown)

Day 311

In that day you will ask Me nothing ... whatever you ask the Father in My name He will give you.
(John 16:23)

Daily reading: Leviticus 4

John, by the Spirit, distinguishes two words for asking. The first in our headline text is a word for asking between two equals. It's always the word Jesus used when asking anything of the Father in prayer, because He was always conscious of His equal dignity with the Father. But the second occurrence in our text is the beggar's word: an asking by someone definitely inferior, and consistently used of our approach to God in prayer. This shows that the first part of verse 23 has nothing to do with prayer, as we'd expect, but is a continuation from verse 19. Is there a sense of awe in our prayer as we lift our face upwards towards our Great Benefactor?

> Sweet hour of prayer! sweet hour of prayer!
> That calls me from a world of care,
> And bids me at my Father's throne
> Make all my wants and wishes known.
> In seasons of distress and grief,
> My soul has often found relief,
> And oft escaped the tempter's snare
> By thy return, sweet hour of prayer!
> (W.W. Walford)

Day 312

The LORD of hosts is with us: The God of Jacob is our refuge.
(Psalm 46:11)

Daily reading: Leviticus 5

Here's one of the great contrasts of God's Word that should thrill our souls. God is "The LORD of hosts", and there's an unlimited number of His angelic host that's all under His authority. "Swiftly they fly at His command, to guard His own of ev'ry land." The high and lofty One who inhabits eternity is also the God of a poor, struggling man like Jacob, and He's not ashamed to be called his God or the God of men and women like him (Heb.11:16). He is our God too, "our refuge and strength, an ever-present help in trouble" (Ps.46:1).

God of our fathers, whose almighty hand
Leads forth in beauty all the starry band
Of shining worlds in splendor through the skies,
Our grateful songs before thy throne arise.
(Daniel C. Roberts)

Day 313

I consider everything a loss because of the surpassing worth of knowing Christ Jesus my Lord. (Philippians 3:8)

Daily reading: Leviticus 6

Christ my Leader, Christ my Peace, Christ hath wrought my soul's release, Christ my Righteousness divine, Christ for me, for He is mine; Christ my Wisdom, Christ my Meat, Christ restores my wandering feet, Christ my Advocate and Priest, Christ who ne'er forgets the least; Christ my Teacher, Christ my Guide, Christ my Rock, in Christ I hide, Christ the Ever-living Bread, Christ His precious Blood hath shed; Christ hath brought me nigh to God, Christ the everlasting Word, Christ my Master, Christ my Head, Christ who for my sins hath bled; Christ my Glory, Christ my Crown, Christ the Plant of great renown, Christ my Comforter on high, Christ my Hope, draws ever nigh (Author unknown).

Day 314

David was a little past the top of the mountain. (2 Samuel 16:1)

Daily reading: Leviticus 7

This is a good verse to share at any older friend's birthday celebration, jokingly suggesting that they're in good company in being a little over the hill! It hadn't been a good day for David. First, there had been Absalom's rebellion, followed by Ahithophel's treason, and now to cap it all, just as he was literally over the top of the hill, news was brought of Mephibosheth's alleged betrayal - and Shimei's curses were still to follow. Surely that was O.T.T. - over the top! Still David could say, 'the Lord will look upon my misery and restore to me his covenant blessing' and he refreshed himself (vv.12,14). If today should prove to be one of those days, and it all gets O.T.T., how do you plan to react?

Day 315

With whom will you compare me or count me equal? To whom will you liken me that we may be compared? (Isaiah 46:5) Who, being in very nature God, did not consider equality with God something to be used to his own advantage. (Philippians 2:6)

Daily reading: Leviticus 8

Adam was in "the likeness of God" (Gen.5:1). Abraham was "the Friend of God" (Jas.2:23). Moses was "the servant of God" (Neh.10:29). David was "the man of God" (Neh.12:24). Haggai and Zechariah were "the prophets of God" (Ezra 5:2). Melchizedek was "the priest of ... God" (Gen.14:18). Each in his own way bore a resemblance to God, but none was equal or compared with Him. Why? because none of them was the Son of God! Only He can compare, for He's the unequalled likeness, Friend, Servant, Man, Prophet and Priest.

Day 316

Noah, a preacher of righteousness. (2 Peter 2:5) God waited ... in the days of Noah. (1 Peter 3:20) God ... wants all people to be saved. (1 Timothy 2:3-4)

Daily reading: Leviticus 9

Noah was God's messenger in a day of unbelief. Even if he hadn't uttered a word, he hammered home the message as he hammered home the nails into the ark. Scoffers and scorners were present, and they saw the ark taking shape. They turned deaf ears, rejecting the good news of deliverance from the judgement to come. Today's environment is fast approaching that of Noah's day. God's grace is extended hourly ... until! Until the Lord comes. Many may have knocked on the closed ark when the rains came, but it was too late. "Today, if you hear his voice, do not harden your hearts" (Heb.3:7,8).

> Come to the ark: the waters rise, the seas their billows rear;
> While darkness gathers o'er the skies, behold a refuge near!
> Come to the ark, all, all that weep beneath the sense of sin:
> Without, deep calleth unto deep, but all is peace within.
> Come to the ark, ere yet the flood your lingering steps oppose;
> Come, for the door which open stood is now about to close.
> (Author unknown)

Day 317

**Let this mind be in you, which was also in Christ Jesus.
(Philippians 2:5 NKJV)
Serving the Lord with all humility of mind. (Acts 20:19 NKJV)**

Daily reading: Leviticus 10

It's in true servanthood that likeness to Christ is most readily, most fully and most wonderfully seen. R.C. Chapman said, 'As a man looking in the mirror sees the counterpart of his own face, so Christ looking at His servant might see the counterpart of His own mind.' May it be in this that we'll earn His highest commendation at His coming.

> With such a blessed hope in view,
> We would more like Him be,
> More like our risen, glorious Lord
> Whose face we soon shall see.
> (Fanny Crosby)

Day 318

**And Hilkiah gave the book to Shaphan, and he read it ...
Shaphan read it before the king. (2 Kings 22:8-11)**

Daily reading: Leviticus 11:1-23

The word 'read' has the thought of 'encountering.' What an encounter it was, firstly for Shaphan himself and then, as he read it a second time, for king Josiah! The order is important - we need a personal encounter with God through the reading of the Word, before doing as Moses did. 'And Moses brought the people out of the camp to meet (from the same word, encounter) with God' (Ex.19:17). Only then can we expect our hearers to do as Josiah did when he 'heard' (this word carries the thought of attention and obedience) and tore his clothes. 'But on this one will I look: on him who is poor and of a contrite spirit, and who trembles at My word' (Is.66:2).

Day 319

**He sent them off to Lebanon in shifts of ten thousand a month, so that they spent one month in Lebanon and two months at home. (1 Kings 5:14)
Come with me by yourselves to a quiet place and get some rest." (Mark 6:31)**

If even the best men of the wisest man couldn't always be in the front line, then we have to realize that sometimes we need a break. The demands of active service for the Lord are great; there must be times of renewal, refreshing, regrouping, reassessing and retraining, otherwise we'll never know the effectiveness of retrenching! But there's another key aspect to Solomon's strategy – it only worked because he'd others available to rotate. Perhaps you can relieve someone today who's on the brink of exhaustion!

> Perhaps the fight would not have been so hard,
> Prepared, I might have faced the fray,
> If I had been alone with Him
> Upon my knees to pray.
> (Author unknown)

Day 320

He is altogether lovely. This is my beloved, this is my friend. (Song of Songs 5:16)

Daily reading: Leviticus 13:1-29

To the artist He's the One Altogether Lovely. To the architect He's the Chief Corner Stone. To the baker He's the Living Bread. To the banker He's the Hidden Treasure. To the biologist He's the Life. To the builder He's the Sure Foundation. To the doctor He's the Great Physician. To the farmer He's the Lord of the Harvest. To the florist He's the Lily of the Valley. To the geologist He's the Rock of Ages. To the jurist He is the Righteous Judge, the Judge of all men. To the jeweler He's the Pearl of Great Price. To the lawyer He's the Advocate. To the horticulturist He's the True Vine. To the oculist He's the Light of the World. Who is Jesus to you? (Author unknown).

Day 321

What kind of work do you do? Where do you come from? What is your country? From what people are you? (Jonah 1:8)

Daily reading: Leviticus 13:30-59

These are still common questions today. People often ask, 'What do you do for a living?' How do you answer? Is your secular employment of greater importance than being a Christian? It would be good to answer, 'I'm a Christian. What's your occupation?' The church in Laodicea had got it wrong. They were trading in the wrong stuff (Rev.3:17,18). Or consider the story the

Lord Jesus told - 'A certain nobleman went into a far country to receive for himself a kingdom and to return. So he called ... his servants, delivering to them ten minas, and said to them, "Do business till I come"' (Lk.19:12,13 NKJV). Isn't this relevant for us today?

I want to be a worker for the Lord;
I want to love and trust his holy word,
I want to sing and pray, and be busy ev'ry day
In the vineyard of the Lord.
I want to be a worker ev'ry day,
I want to lead the erring in the way
That leads to heav'n above, where all is peace and love,
In the kingdom of the Lord.
I want to be a worker strong and brave,
I want to trust in Jesus' pow'r to save,
All who will truly come, shall find a happy home,
In the kingdom of the Lord.
I want to be a worker, help me Lord,
To lead the lost and erring to thy word,
That points to joys on high, where pleasures never die,
In the kingdom of the Lord.
(Isaiah Baltzell)

Day 322

Simeon and Levi are brothers; instruments of cruelty are in their dwelling place ... Cursed be their anger, for it is fierce; and their wrath, for it is cruel! (Genesis 49:5-7).

Daily reading: Leviticus 14:1-29

The election of Aaron and his sons to the priesthood of Israel was a surprising act of divine sovereignty given Jacob's grim curse of their tribe. The curse was changed to the Mosaic blessing: "Bless his substance, Lord, and accept the work of his hands ..." (Deut.33:11). So it's been with us. Divine grace has worked with and in "children of wrath" to fulfil God's elective purposes. We've been brought near, blessed to share in divine service and called upon to offer our bodies as instruments of righteousness (Rom.6:13 NKJV).

A mind at perfect peace with God, oh! what a word is this!
A sinner reconciled through blood; This, this indeed is peace!
By nature and by practice far, how very far from God;
Yet now by grace brought nigh to Him, through faith in Jesus' blood.
So near, so very near to God, I cannot nearer be;
For in the person of His Son I am as near as He.
(Horatius Bonar)

Day 323

Follow Me. (Matthew 4:19)
...take up their cross and follow Me. (Matthew 16:24)
Levi ... left everything and followed Him. (Luke 5:28)

Daily reading: Leviticus 14:30-57

If I gained the world, but not the Saviour,
Were my life worth living for a day?
Could my yearning heart find rest and comfort
In the things that soon must pass away?
If I gained the world, but not the Saviour,
Would my gain be worth the life-long strife?
Are all earthly pleasures worth comparing
For a moment with a Christ-filled life?
(A. Olander)

Christ or the world? Solid rock or sinking sand? Peace or discord? Eternal life or eternal loss? What will your answer be?

Day 324

Safety is of the LORD. (Proverbs 21:31 KJV)
Hold me up, and I shall be safe. (Psalm 119:117 NKJV)

Daily reading: Leviticus 15

"Safe" is the most assuring and comforting word to the ear of the anxious, whether it be about the restored patient, the lost traveller or the endangered worker. But it's more wonderful when it's used to describe the believing sinner. No wonder Rupert Brooke could write in his poem, 'Safety', during the First World War:

Safe shall be my going,
Secretly armed against all death's endeavour,
Safe though all safety's lost; safe where men fall;
And if these poor limbs die, safest of all.

Day 325

... the Spirit Himself makes intercession for us with groanings which cannot be uttered. (Romans 8:26 NJKV)

The word 'intercession' can convey a range of ideas. It can mean to come across someone in trouble and to plead for that person. Or it can simply be to meet with someone and to engage in bold, familiar communion. As you meet with God today and enjoy close communion, perhaps your attention will be drawn to someone who's standing in need of prayer right now. What are you going to pray for them? Well, when the Lord prayed for others in John 17, His concern was for their unity, joy, protection, dedication, witness and the experience of His presence.

> Arise, my soul, arise! Shake off thy guilty fears;
> The bleeding Sacrifice in my behalf appears.
> Before the throne my Surety stands;
> My name is written on his hands.
> He ever lives above, for me to intercede,
> His all-redeeming love, his precious blood to plead.
> His blood atoned for all our race,
> And sprinkles now the throne of grace.
> (Charles Wesley)

Day 326

But Jesus said, 'Someone touched me; I know that power has gone out from me.' (Luke 8:46)

Daily reading: Leviticus 17

"Out from me' - He never came, like others, to demonstrate power through things that were extensions of themselves. He had no rod, no jaw-bone of an ass, no ox-goad, no sling, no sword. He picked up nothing from this world to manifest His might: He brought it with Him from above. His virtue was within. Out from Him on the way to Calvary came the virtue of His touch, the virtue of His word, even the virtue of His spittle. Then, on the cross, out of Him came the virtue of His blood.

> And still they come, a multitude, each burdened by his sin;
> And still they own with gratitude – "His virtue is within."
> (Mary A. Lathbury)

Day 327

The Son is the radiance of God's glory and the exact representation of his being, sustaining all things by his powerful word. (Hebrews 1:3)

Daily reading: Leviticus 18

To the philanthropist He's the unspeakable Gift. To the philosopher He's the Wisdom of God. To the sculptor He's the Living Stone. To the servant He's the Good Master. To the statesman He's the Desire of All Nations. To the student He's the Incarnate Truth. To the theologian He's the Author and Finisher of Our Faith. To the traveler He's the New and Living Way. To the toiler He's the Giver of Rest. To the sinner He's the Lamb of God that takes away the sin of the world. To the Christian He's the Son of the Living God, the Saviour, the Redeemer and Lord.

Day 328

Therefore we must give the more earnest heed to the things we have heard, lest we should drift away. (Hebrews 2:1)

Daily reading: Leviticus 19

Have you noticed how the car driver spots more interesting things than the front seat passenger? Why is that? Perhaps it's obvious that concern for safety will increase the driver's attentiveness. As a passenger, the scenery might even fade into a blur as you speed along. This life is full of spiritual points of interest. If we're attentive, we'll spot them. However, it's all too easy to let them all flow by without noticing. The driver looks for things that are unexpected. The driver's eye is trained by experience, and the unusual attracts attention – both productive paths and potential pitfalls. Spiritual experience based on the knowledge and application of Scripture is a 'must.' It teaches us what to look for, and what to stand for, in Christian life. Don't just be a sleepy passenger – be alert at the wheel.

Day 329

I am full of heaviness; I looked for someone to take pity, but there was none; And for comforters, but I found none. (Psalm 69:20 NKJV)

In a full ministry, the One who is full of grace and truth delivered men who were full of leprosy and full of sores; he described some as being full of extortion, hypocrisy and iniquity; and he dispensed blessing in full waterpots, baskets and nets. On the cross, he was fully ready to give Himself, and He was full of heaviness, knowing that the heavy judgement of God for our sin was about to be laid on Him. In such a state, they brought Him vinegar to drink - in a full vessel, in a full sponge. In their wickedness, they showed no half measure. In His goodness, neither did He.

Day 330

Cleanse me ... wash me. (Psalm 51:7)
Restore to me the joy of your salvation. (Psalm 51:12)
Sinners will turn back to you. (Psalm 51:13)

Daily reading: Leviticus 21

David's prayer (v.8) was literally something like please 'make my bones to dance'! From the flow of the psalm we learn that earnest prayer precedes joyful renewal which, in turn, results in sinners being brought to repentance. Is anything more infectious than joy? Could there be a truer advert for Christianity than Christians expressing the real joy that accompanies salvation? If we've lost that joy, let's make regaining it a matter of earnest prayer. Revivals begin in the hearts of God's children.

Revive thy work, O Lord, thy mighty arm make bare;
Speak with the voice that wakes the dead, first make thy people hear.
Revive thy work, O Lord, disturb this sleep of death;
Quicken the smould'ring embers now by thine almighty breath.
Revive thy work, O Lord, create soul-thirst for thee;
And hung'ring for the Bread of Life O may our spirits be.
(Albert Midlane)

Day 331

Remember your Creator in the days of your youth.
(Ecclesiastes 12:1)

Daily reading: Leviticus 22

A man came rushing breathlessly up to a ferry. He got there just as the gateman shut the doors in his face. Someone standing by remarked, 'I'm afraid you didn't run fast enough.' The disappointed traveller replied, 'I ran fast enough, but I'm afraid I didn't start early enough.' Be encouraged, young friend. To accomplish the most for your Master you should start out early.

> In the glad morning of my day,
> My life to give, my vows to pay,
> With no reserve and no delay,
> With all my heart, I come.
> (Marianne Farningham)

Day 332

Carry each other's burdens, and in this way you will fulfill the law of Christ. (Galatians 6:2)

Daily reading: Leviticus 23:1-22

Martha was burdened with serving Jesus, and she asked the Lord to tell Mary to help her carry the load. Jesus would do no such thing! The word used in Luke 10:40 indicates she was dragging her cares around – and they were not necessary cares. If Mary had shared the burden, she'd also have been distracted from something far more important – a case of a problem shared being a problem doubled, not halved! Jesus' advice wasn't to carry it but to cut it loose. There are times when others carry a burden that's necessary and unavoidable and, if we can, we must reduce their load by taking some of it from them. At other times, the burden is self-inflicted and a distraction from higher priorities. Gently advising to 'cut loose' will also fulfil the law of Christ, won't it?

> Have you had a kindness shown? Pass it on, pass it on!
> 'Twas not giv'n for thee alone, Pass it on, pass it on!
> Let it travel down the years, let it wipe another's tears;
> Till in heav'n the deed appears, Pass it on, pass it on!
> Live for self, you live in vain;
> Live for Christ, you live again,
> Live for Him, with Him you reign.
> Pass it on, pass it on!
> (Henry Burton)

Day 333

You come to the help of those who gladly do right, who remember your ways. But when we continued to sin against them, you were angry. How then can we be saved? (Isaiah 64:5)

Daily reading: Leviticus 23:23-44

Moses was a wise man. He wanted the people to know that there are no dead ends in the ways of God. The lamb was the way out; the dried river was the way through; meeting God was the way forward; the veil was the way in. So it is for the Christian. The journey which began by faith at the cross, to which we testified in our baptism, continues daily by meeting God and culminates within the veil in heavenly worship. What a wonderful way to travel homeward! And what of our final arrival there and that long-awaited meeting? The Lord Himself shall descend from heaven… and we shall be caught up in the clouds TO MEET THE LORD in the air.

Come, thou long expected Jesus, born to set Thy people free;
From our fears and sins release us; let us find our rest in Thee
Israel's Strength and Consolation, hope of all the earth Thou art;
Dear Desire of every nation, Joy of every longing heart
(Charles Wesley)

Day 334

If one part suffers, every part suffers with it; if one part is honored, every part rejoices with it. (1 Corinthians 12:26)

Daily reading: Leviticus 24

Laugh and the world laughs with you; weep and you weep alone; this grand old earth must borrow its mirth, it has troubles enough of its own. Sing, and the hills will answer; sigh, it is lost on the air; the echoes bound to a joyful sound but shrink from voicing care. Be glad, and your friends are many; be sad, and you lose them all; There are none to decline your nectared wine, but alone you must drink life's gall. There is room in the halls of pleasure for a long and lovely train, but one by one we must all file in through the narrow aisles of pain. Rejoice and men will seek you; grieve and they turn and go— they want full measure of your pleasure, but they do not want your woe. (Ella Wheeler Wilcox)

Here's an opportunity to show the world that Christ makes a difference in how we treat each other.

Day 335

And he died for all, that those who live should no longer live for themselves but for him who died for them and was raised again. (2 Corinthians 5:15)

Daily reading: Leviticus 25:1-24

It's gloriously true that "Christ died for our sins" but here's a further marvellous truth - that He died for our lives too. Believer, are you living for yourself? What a bitter disappointment for Him to see lives for which He died being squandered in pointless, personal pursuits when they could be constrained to conquering commitment to Christ.

> Jesus, Master, whose I am, purchased Thine alone to be,
> By Thy blood, O spotless Lamb, shed so willingly for me;
> Let my heart be all Thine own, let me live to Thee alone.
> (Frances Ridley Havergal)

Day 336

... since you are his child, God has made you also an heir. (Galatians 4:7)

Daily reading: Leviticus 25:25-55

Turning frogs into princes is the stuff of fairytales. The reality of God's transformation is far more stupendous. He makes saints out of sinners. He lifts paupers to princely glory. More importantly He robes the helpless in garments of salvation. He takes the mourning and brings them into wedding joy. He translates those sitting in the power of darkness into the kingdom of the Son of His love. Nor should any of us Christians think that we are made just bystanders in the heavenly procession; we are heirs. How rich is God? Look at the glorious answer to all the sufferings of the Son. We enter into an inheritance that dazzles the eyes, captivates the mind and thrills the soul. Put down the fiction - the reality is so much better!

> Sons of God, belovèd in Jesus! O the wondrous word of grace;
> In His Son the Father sees us, and as sons He gives us place.
> Blessèd hope now brightly beaming, on our God we soon shall gaze;
> And in light celestial gleaming, we shall see our Savior's face.
> By the power of grace transforming, we shall then His image bear;
> Christ His promised word performing, we shall then His glory share.
> (D.W. Whittle)

Day 337

And the Lord added to the church daily those who were being saved. (Acts 2:47)

Daily reading: Leviticus 26:1-26

This was God's Pentecostal arithmetic. The person of Christ had become the greatest plus in thousands of lives and He wanted them to be a plus for Him. What a binding of Christians! What a building of that church! Jerusalem was on fire for God. Is your town? Is your church? Are you? Or has distraction and subtraction spoiled the intended impact and the continuing expectation of 'the Lord added'?

> The church that hopes to win the lost
> Must pay the one unchanging cost;
> She must compel the world to see
> In her the Christ of Calvary.
> (Author unknown)

Day 338

.... treacherous, rash, conceited, lovers of pleasure rather than lovers of God ... having a form of godliness but denying its power. (2 Timothy 3:4)

Daily reading: Leviticus 26:27-46

Love of self is a denial of Him, and love of Him is the denial of self. He's spoken to us in that stimulating love of His to be losers in time and keepers in eternity. Tragically, if we choose to be keepers now, we will be losers then – in fact, we'll also be losers now. Jim Elliot was right: 'He is no fool who gives what he cannot keep to gain that which he cannot lose.'

> Just think for a moment, it isn't your own,
> It belongs to the One whose Lordship you own,
> But He gives it to you on permanent loan,
> So USE it; don't LOSE it as treasure in heaven.
> (Author unknown)

Day 339

And do not grieve the Holy Spirit of God, with whom you were sealed for the day of redemption. (Ephesians 4:30)

'Grieve' is a 'love' word. We may hurt or anger someone who has no affection for us but we can only grieve a person who loves us. Paul writes in Romans 15:30 about the love of the Spirit. He's the Spirit of truth, faith, grace and holiness. We must therefore be diligent in these things and ensure our conduct is Christlike, otherwise His ministry may be suspended from our lives.

> May we His holy strivings know,
> And to His voice give heed;
> So by Him live and walk and grow,
> As sons of God indeed.
> (Cecil Belton)

Day 340

'Sir,' the man replied, 'leave it alone for one more year, and I'll dig around it and fertilize it.' (Luke 13:8)

Daily reading: Ezra 1

Pruners should be among every gardener's tools; patience should be among his traits. The vineyard owner thought three years of fruitlessness was enough. His gardener asked for another year. How grateful we are that, despite past failure, the Lord in His patience gave us "this year also." When involved in spiritual restoration, we, too, need a "spirit of meekness" (Gal.6:1 NKJV). Try more fertilising before felling.

> Judge not too fast. This tree that does appear
> So barren, may be fruitful the next year.
> Thy judgment oft may tread beside the text;
> A Saul today, may prove a Paul the next.
> (Author unknown)

Day 341

Better a patient person than a warrior, one with self-control than one who takes a city. (Proverbs 16:32)

Daily reading: Ezra 2

David enjoyed military successes, but our text indicates his meekness under provocation was more important to God. Perhaps thinking of Eliab (1 Sam.17:28), Absalom (2 Sam.15:4) and Shimei (2 Sam.16:7,8), he wrote of

tongues 'like a sharp razor', and words like 'drawn swords.' We're not called
'to be quick on the draw', but 'slow to anger' and 'slow to speak.'

Lord, search us, lest in wordy zeal
We hide the Christ we would reveal,
Or cloud, by jealous argument,
the very truth we represent.
Lord, keep us true, but ever kind,
with Thine own gentleness of mind,
With Thine own 'wisdom from above'
Whose strongest argument is LOVE.
(J. Sidlow Baxter)

Day 342

**So he ran ahead and climbed a sycamore-fig tree to see him,
since Jesus was coming that way.
(Luke 19:4)**

Daily reading: Ezra 3

Perhaps Jesus had used sycamore wood in Joseph's carpentry shop. It's a light
and durable wood but its strength on the day Luke records was its ability to
take the weight of Zacchaeus. Not all short people are lightweights! The
'sycamore' in Israel produces figs, not horse-chestnuts to play 'conkers' with.
What a worthy, useful tree, and what a contrast to the person who clambered
into its branches. It was, though, a picture of the Man below, who'd grown in
wisdom and stature, and was able also to meet the immense need of the
spiritually impoverished tax collector. He can meet our needs too. At least
Zacchaeus had the good sense to hurry to improve his knowledge of Christ. Is
it your job today, sycamore-like, to support someone else in gaining a better
view of Christ?

Zaccheus climbed the tree, and thought himself unknown:
But how surprised was he, when Jesus called him down!
The Lord beheld him, though concealed,
And by a word his power revealed.
Wonder and joy at once were painted in His face;
"Does He my name pronounce, and does He know my case?"
Will Jesus deign with me to dine? Lord, I, with all I have, am Thine.
Thus, where the gospel's preached, and sinners come to hear,
The hearts of some are reached before they are aware:
The word directly speaks to them and seems to point them out by name.
'Tis curiosity oft brings them in the way,

Only the Man to see and hear what He can say;
But how the sinner starts to find, the Preacher knows his inmost mind.
His long-forgotten thoughts are brought again in view,
And all his secret thoughts revealed in public too,
Though compassed with a crowd about,
The searching word has found him out.
While this distressing pain and sorrow fills the heart,
He hears a voice again that bids his fear's depart;
Then like Zaccheus he is blessed and Jesus deigns to be his guest.
(John Newton)

Day 343

**He reigned ... and to no one's sorrow, departed.
(2 Chronicles 21:20 NKJV)
He shall be buried with the burial of an ass. (Jeremiah 22:19)**

Daily reading: Ezra 4

Unwanted and unclean, two kings ended their days, both cases of justifiable rejection. The reference to the burial of an ass is intended to be ironic, because typically an ass wasn't thought worthy of a burial but dragged aside to rot and be pecked apart by unclean scavengers. The two men stirred no sense of joy in their lives, or tears in their death; there was no sense of glory, and there was no sense of grief either. Sadly, our Saviour was rejected, too; He was abandoned as unwanted on the cross and was to be buried as unclean until a secret disciple abandoned his secrecy and gave a spotless tomb for the spotless Lamb.

Jesus from the tomb has come, death to Him could do no harm;
Comforted let us remain, and together praise His name.
Now redemption's work is done, all His foes He's overcome.
Once for all our sins He bore, Now He'll suffer nevermore.
From the grain of wheat that died, many grains were multiplied;
He no more alone abides, all the church is at His side.
As His Body, with our Head, to the heavens we'll ascend;
With Him buried, with Him soar, praise His name forevermore.
(Author unknown)

Day 344

**God ... devises means so that His banished ones are not
expelled from Him. (2 Samuel 14:14 NKJV)**

The woman who said this was described by God as being wise. Perhaps she didn't fully realize it, but in this one short sentence she summarized the story of our redemption. Sin had banished us from God's presence, but thankfully not without hope, for God found a way for banished ones to be brought back. How? He devised means; literally, He thought thoughts, and they were thoughts of holiness and of love; thoughts of righteousness and of grace. And His thoughts found their wonderful outworking at Calvary where the Saviour offered one sacrifice for sins for ever. And now "Jerusalem's bright gates are standing open; Go to the banished ones and fetch them in" (Mrs Pennefather).

O God, whose thoughts are brightest light, Whose love always runs clear,
To whose kind wisdom sinning souls amidst their sins are dear,
How Thou can'st think so well of us, yet be the God Thou art,
Is darkness to my intellect, but sunshine to my heart.
(Frederick W. Faber)

Day 345

They forgot the God who saved them. (Psalm 106:21)
They soon forgot what he had done. (Psalm 106:13)
Forget not all His benefits. (Psalm 103:2)

Daily reading: Ezra 6

"Lord, I shall be very busy this day, I may forget Thee, but do not Thou forget me." We assume the pressures of life are limited to the twenty-first century but Sir Jacob Astley wrote this in the eleventh! Almost a thousand years later his prayer's still valid. Israel was warned, "Be careful that you do not forget the Lord your God" (Deut.8:11), but they did; and so do we. We forget all His benefits and blessings. We fume, despair, complain and groan because we forget His claim on our lives. Parents lament when their children forget or ignore their advice. We fall into the same trap. Instead let's tune into David's advice to, "Praise the Lord, my soul, and forget not all his benefits ... who forgives ... heals ... redeems ... satisfies" (Ps.103:2-5).

God reigns on high, but ne'er confines His goodness to the skies;
Through the whole earth His bounty shines, and every want supplies.
Creatures with all their endless race, Thy power and praise proclaim;
But saints, who taste Thy richer grace, delight to bless Thy Name.
(Isaac Watts)

Day 346

Do not quench the Spirit. (1 Thessalonians 5:19)

Daily reading: Ezra 7

Like grieving the Spirit, quenching Him is a sin committed by believers in Christ. To quench is to 'put out' or to 'put a damper on.' When we quench the Spirit we 'put the fire out.' This doesn't mean we expel Him, but that we extinguish His love and power as He seeks to carry out His divine purpose through us. Someone has said, 'Resist not His incoming; grieve not His indwelling; quench not His outgoing.'

> Try us, O God! and know our thoughts,
> Cleanse Thou our hearts from secret sin;
> So shall our lives be pure without, our souls be pure within.
> (Author unknown)

Day 347

Jesus ... departed ... to a mountain by Himself. (John 6:15)
The Teacher ... is calling for you. (John 11:28)

Daily reading: Ezra 8

There are two major challenges to any 'Quiet Time' with the Lord these days – finding the time, then finding the quiet! We need them to survive. The Lord had His mountain and His garden. David had his cave, Daniel his room and Elijah his brook. What about you? Seek and you shall find if you are determined to set aside time for emptying and refilling the mind, restoring the soul, and renewing strength. The benefits and blessings will be yours. Others will benefit from you later.

> When storms of life are round me beating,
> When rough the path that I have trod,
> Within my closet door retreating, I love to be alone with God.
> 'Tis there I find new strength for duty, as o'er the sands of time I plod;
> I see the king in all His beauty, while resting there alone with God.
> Alone with God, the world forbidden, Alone with God, O blest retreat!
> Alone with God, and in Him hidden, to hold with Him communion sweet.
> (Johnson Oatman)

Day 348

The eyes of everyone ... were fastened on Him ... All ... were amazed at the gracious words that came from His lips. (Luke 4:20,22)

Daily reading: Ezra 9

The people in the synagogue were looking and listening. They found nothing incompatible in what Jesus did and what He said. It will be important for your walk and talk to be synchronised today. Don't allow what you do to drown out what you say.

You must be true yourself if you the truth would teach;
Your soul must overflow if you another's soul would reach!
It needs the overflow of heart to give the lips full speech.
Think truly, and your thoughts shall the world's famine feed;
Speak truly, and each word of yours shall be a fruitful seed;
Live truly, and your life shall be a great and noble creed.
(Horatius Bonar)

Day 349

Like arrows in the hands of a warrior are children born in one's youth. (Psalm 127:4)

Daily reading: Ezra 10

The arrows in the quiver are taken one by one by the archer at the appropriate time and placed in the bow. His strength holds them securely and he takes aim. Every arrow has a target and a purpose. The archer's greatest desire is to hit the target by the strength of his arm and the carefulness of his aim. He watches his arrows carefully until they strike home. Do we have enough spiritual strength to hold our children securely? Do we have we the right target for them and do we take carefully measured aim? As we let go, do we cover their progress watchfully with prayer so that they may reach the target? Or is there a danger, in spiritual terms, of their failure to launch?

Day 350

I am the LORD in the midst. (Exodus 8:22)
... and among the lampstands was someone like a son of man. (Revelation 1:13)

Sitting in the midst of the doctors (Lk.2:46)
Stooping in the midst of the Pharisees (Jn 8:1-8)
Stepping into the boat in the midst of the sea (Mk.6:45-51)
Suffering in the midst of the malefactors (Jn 19:18)
Standing in the midst of the heavenly throng (Rev.5:6-13)
Singing in the midst of the congregation (Heb.2:12, Ps.22:22)

Of the vast universe of bliss
The centre He and sun;
Th' eternal theme of praise is this:
God's well-beloved One,
Worthy the name of Jesus now,
That every knee therein should bow.
(Josiah Conder)

Day 351

Bezalel ... made the lampstand of pure gold.
(Exodus 37:1,17 NKJV)

Daily reading: Psalm 52

When Bezalel began his laborious task, he probably had a slab of gold that was around thirty kilograms in weight. From this he beat (which means moulded by hammering) the lampstand for the tabernacle. What a job of patient love that was! Each separate tap of the hammer would produce little, if any, discernible effect, but the cumulative result was an article of furniture of consummate beauty with its shaft, branches, bowls and flowers. Are you busy in some work for the Lord, gently tapping away with the hammer of the Word, but with each class, each house-meeting, each letter showing little noticeable effect? Keep your confidence that 'Your labour is not vain in the Lord' (1 Cor.15:58).

Another year of labor, and labor not in vain;
For while the seed we've planted, God gave the promised rain.
His love has been our comfort, His strength has been our stay,
Hold fast His hand, march onward, still trusting day by day.
O blessed, blessed harvest of souls for Christ our King,
When we who toil in weakness with joy our fruit shall bring.
Then let us not be weary, but work and watch and pray;
Hold fast His hand, march onward, still trusting day by day.
(Fanny J. Crosby)

Day 352

Since no one knows the future, who can tell someone else what is to come? (Ecclesiastes 8:7)

Daily reading: Psalm 53

God can – but if he doesn't, that doesn't mean we should be concerned. 'The oriental shepherd was always ahead of his sheep. He was down in front. Any attack on them had to take Him into account. Now God is down in front. He is in the tomorrows. It is tomorrow that fills men with dread. God is there already. All the tomorrows of our life have to pass Him before they can get to us.' (F.B. Meyer)

God is in every tomorrow, therefore I live for today:
Certain of finding at sunrise guidance and strength for the day,
Power for each moment of weakness, hope for each moment of pain,
Comfort for every sorrow, sunshine and joy after rain.
(Author Unknown)

Day 353

Away with Him. (John 19:15)
Away with him. (Acts 21:36)

Daily reading: Psalm 54

Attitudes hadn't changed and, for the people of Jerusalem, Paul was too much like his Saviour. Actions hadn't changed either and their cry, "Away with him", was an echo of the cross. In fact, the word used for 'away' means to raise, to take up, or to lift. Nothing's changed - the more Christlike you become, the more different you are from the world, and the more likely you are to be rejected; the less Christlike you become the more likely you are to blend in with the world and leave it strangely untouched. One of the greatest proofs of the effectiveness of Christian life and ministry is when this hostile world cries, "Away with them." But if it's silent, it's probably because it's us who are effectively saying we're "away with them."

"Away with Him! Away with Him!" The scornful rabble cried,
And mocked, rejected, long ago, our Lord was crucified.
"Away with Him! Away with Him!"
How many cry today who will not head his loving call,
But, careless, turn away!
"Away with Him! Away with Him!" How hard the heart must be
To pass, unmoved, that blood-stained cross upon Mount Calvary!

(Maud Frazer Jackson)

Day 354

When he was at the table with them, he took bread, gave thanks, broke it and began to give it to them. (Luke 24:30)

Daily reading: Psalm 55

Our modern rules of etiquette were certainly breached here! What would we think if a guest to our table took charge of the proceedings and distributed the food? Perhaps this was a clue that here was no ordinary travelling companion. The way He spoke to God so intimately would have been a further hint. But what opened their eyes? Surely it was when He started to give the bread to them. They couldn't have missed the nail-wounded hands and so all became clear. Just a glimpse of His hands today, still wounded, will have a similar effect - we'll see Jesus in a new light as well.

Crown him the Lord of love; behold his hands and side,
Rich wounds, yet visible above, in beauty glorified;
No angels in the sky can fully bear that sight,
But downward bends their burning eye
At mysteries so bright.
(Matthew Bridges)

Day 355

**Walk in obedience to all that the Lord your God has commanded you, so that you may live and prosper and prolong your days in the land that you will possess.
(Deuteronomy 5:33)**

Daily reading: Psalm 56

Upward and forward your path plan today,
Attaining fresh heights as you walk Jesus' way;
Ignore past failures, but work for the prize,
Striving for goals fit for His holy eyes.
Not, 'how did he die?' but 'how did he live?'
Not, 'what did he gain?' but 'what did he give?'
These are the merits to measure the worth
Of a man as a man, regardless of birth.
Not, 'what was his status?' but 'had he a heart?'
And 'how did he play his God-given part?'
(Author Unknown)

Day 356

I consider everything a loss because of the surpassing worth of knowing Christ Jesus my Lord ... (Philippians 3:8)

Daily reading: Psalm 57

The rich young man preferred his possessions (Mk.10:22), the Gadarenes preferred their pigs (Lk.8:37), and Demas preferred this present world (2 Tim.4:10). What's your priority? Will the Lord's voice and hand (S.of S.5:2,4) move you to a prompt response or will you allow Him to depart (S.of S.5:6)?

> And Christ went sadly, He had wrought for them a sign
> Of love, and hope, and tenderness divine; They wanted - swine.
> Christ stands without your door and gently knocks;
> But if your gold or swine the entrance blocks,
> He forces no man's hold - He will depart,
> And leave you to the treasures of your heart.
> (John Oxenham)

Day 357

He shall see of the travail of His soul and shall be satisfied: by His knowledge shall My Righteous Servant justify many; for He shall bear their iniquities. (Isaiah 53:11)

Daily reading: Psalm 58

Worship is kindled in our hearts as we consider these five couplets: suffering and satisfaction, sin and justification, knowledge and foreknowledge, Father and Servant, sinner and sacrifice. The Lord knew that the Cross was the only means of our justification, and He foreknew that it was the only means of His satisfaction. With joy we anticipate the moment when we shall see Him, when Saviour and saved shall speak the single word - "satisfied" (Ps.17:15)!

> So shall it be at last, in that bright morning,
> When the soul waketh, and life's shadows flee;
> O in that hour, fairer than daylight dawning,
> Shall rise the glorious thought, I am with Thee.
> (Author unknown)

Day 358

Who dares despise the day of small things? (Zechariah 4:10)

How often do we feel that what we're involved in is too small to be effective? Sometimes, it seems that our efforts are just a drop in the bucket; but the bucket gets wetter! It has always been God's way. Take, for example, His dealings with Israel of old, only a small people in comparison to the nations of the world, but He fulfilled His purposes in them in their day. Don't despise small things - many of the great spiritual revivals over the years were started by small groups of believers with a clear and gripping vision of God's will. Smallness does have its advantages – it can allow us to be nimble, it keeps us humble and it keeps us relying on God to do what we can't. Don't be discouraged - just focus your vision!

> Little drops of water, little grains of sand,
> Make the mighty ocean and the beauteous land.
> Little seeds of mercy sown by youthful hands,
> Grow to bless the nations far in other lands.
> (Julia Abigail Carney)

Day 359

… and to know this love that surpasses knowledge—that you may be filled to the measure of all the fullness of God. (Ephesians 3:19)

Daily reading: Psalm 60

A young child enjoying a day at the beach was filling his bucket with seawater. When he was asked what he was doing, he replied, 'I'm putting the sea into my bucket'! That's like us with the love of Christ. His love is like a shoreless ocean and the best – and the best thing - we can do is to fill our tiny hearts until they're overflowing. But speaking of buckets reminds us of the old song about the boy who had a hole in his – in that condition it could contain nothing of any value. Forgive the pun, but unless there's holiness there'll be a hole in us!

> It passeth knowledge, that dear love of Thine,
> My Savior, Jesus; yet this soul of mine
> Would of Thy love in all its breadth and length,
> Its height and depth, its everlasting strength, know more and more.
> Oh, fill me, holy Saviour, with Thy love;
> Lead, lead me to the living fount above.
> Thither may I in simple faith draw nigh,
> And never to another fountain fly, but unto Thee.
> (Mary Shekleton)

Day 360

And there were ... shepherds ... keeping watch ... by night. And ... the angel of the Lord came upon them, and the glory of the Lord shone round about them ... (Luke 2:8,9 NKJV)

Daily reading: Psalm 61

The Greek words for 'keeping watch' associate with a military squadron guarding against threats. But here was a heavenly squadron that might have first seemed threatening until they explained their mission. There was no need for fear because it was a message of unspeakable joy, a declaration of the love of God for fallen mankind. "Today in the town of David a Saviour has been born to you; he is the Messiah, the Lord" (Luke 2:11). What a revelation! The news warmed the hearts of the shepherds so much that they went AWOL (absent without leave) and hastened to Bethlehem to see for themselves. Any lukewarmness in our hearts will soon vanish if we, like the shepherds, by faith gaze in the manger and see afresh the wonder of the gift of God: Immanuel, God with us.

All hail to Thee, Immanuel,
We cast our crowns before Thee;
Let ev'ry heart obey Thy will,
And ev'ry voice adore Thee.
In praise to Thee, our Savior King,
The vibrant chords of Heaven ring,
And echo back the mighty strain:
All hail! All hail! Immanuel!
(D.R. Van Sickle)

Day 361

The shepherds returned, glorifying and praising God for all the things they had heard and seen, which were just as they had been told. (Luke 2:20)

Daily reading: Psalm 62

As the shepherds hurried towards Bethlehem, their hearts would be filled with wonder after receiving the angelic message. But, was there perhaps some element of doubt lurking in their minds? Had the long promised Saviour really been born that very night? Was it really true that the One from heaven was lying in a manger? With eager and perhaps with trembling anticipation they came and what joy when they found it all "just as they had been told." How else could it be? The promises of God delivered over the ages must certainly come to pass. As we considered yesterday, let's go in faith to that manger and gaze upon the wonderful sight. Then, like the shepherds, we'll glorify and praise God.

> Celebrate Immanuel's name, the Prince of life and peace.
> God with us, our lips proclaim, our faithful hearts confess.
> God is in our flesh revealed; heav'n and earth in Jesus join.
> Mortal with Immortal filled, and human with divine.
> (Charles Wesley)

Day 362

**But when you pray, go into your room, close the door...
(Matthew 6:6)**

Daily reading: Psalm 63

Lord, I have shut the door, speak now the word, which in the din and throng could not be heard; hushed now my inner heart, whisper Thy will, while I have come apart, while all is still.

Lord, I have shut the door, here do I bow; speak, for my soul attent turns to Thee now. Rebuke Thou what is vain, counsel my soul, Thy holy will reveal, my will control. In this blest quietness clamorings cease; here in Thy presence dwells infinite peace; yonder, the strife and cry, yonder, the sin.

Lord, I have shut the door, Thou art within! Lord, I have shut the door, strengthen my heart; yonder awaits the task—I share a part. Only through grace bestowed may I be true; here, while alone with Thee, my strength renew.
(William White Runyan)

Day 363

**And in the morning came the word of the LORD unto me.
(Ezekiel 12:8)
Very early in the morning, while it was still dark, Jesus got up,
left the house and went off to a solitary place, where he prayed.
(Mark 1:35)**

Daily reading: Psalm 64

Do you practice the habit of doing business with your God before the busy-ness of your day? The Best of all servants left us this example: begin the day with God, then face its opportunities and difficulties together. There's always a danger that we will close the day with a closed ear, if we didn't open the day with an opened ear.

> I sought the Lord in the morning when the day was at its best,
> And His presence came like sunrise, like a glory in my breast.
> So I think I know the secret learned through many a weary way,
> If you seek Him in the morning you will keep Him through the day.
> (F.I. Howell)

Day 364

The butler and the baker of the king of Egypt. (Genesis 40:5)
Jesus took bread ... and He took the cup. (Matthew 26:26,27)

Daily reading: Psalm 65

Events followed even as Joseph had foretold. The baker, the man who handled the bread, was sentenced to death; while the butler, the man who handled the cup, was exalted again to his place. The Man who handled the bread and the cup in the upper room was sentenced to death, but three days later was restored to life. This was all as the Scriptures had foretold.

> This broken bread and poured-out wine
> Sweet hallowed memories enshrine
> Of that great sacrifice divine - Jesus, our Lord.
> (Charles Mann Luxmoore)

Day 365

A great door ... is opened unto me. (1 Corinthians 16:9)
And pray for us, too, that God may open a door for our
message, so that we may proclaim the mystery of Christ.
(Colossians 4:3)

Daily reading: Psalm 66

Doors in Scripture can indicate the means of redemption (Israel's blood-spattered doors during Passover – see Ex.12:7); a sign of rejection (Laodicea's closed door to the Lord – see Rev.3:20); the entrance of salvation ("I am the door" – see Jn 10:9) and the seal of protection (Noah and family shut in the ark – see Gen.7:16). Today's texts speak of a great and effectual door of opportunity for the Scriptures in Ephesus which enemies sought to close; Paul asking for prayer for open doors of declamation elsewhere for declaring the mystery of Christ; and thirdly, a door for dedication where, typically, our ears are bored to the door as willing bondservants, indicating we're His for our lifetime.

The Lord has set before us
A wide and open door;
And all may enter in there,
And none may shut it more.
It leads to realms of beauty,
Out from the depths of sin;
It turns on golden hinges,
And all may enter in.
(O.D. Sherman)

Day 366

Wine is a mocker and beer a brawler; whoever is led astray by them is not wise. (Proverbs 20:1)

Daily reading: Psalm 67

Millions rely on alcohol to help them bring in the New Year – and then get them through it. Yet, Evangeline Cory Booth said, 'Drink has drained more blood, sold more houses, armed more villains, slain more children, snapped more wedding rings, defiled more innocents, blinded more eyes, twisted more limbs, dethroned more reasons, wrecked more manhood, dishonoured more womanhood, broken more hearts, driven more to suicide than any other scourge that ever swept across the world.' Rather than end the year on a dour note, let's recall that the fruit of the Spirit is never fermented, while thanking God that we're not relying on Jack Daniel's bourbon but God's blessing to see us through!

ABOUT THE PUBLISHER

Hayes Press (www.hayespress.org) is a registered charity in the United Kingdom, whose primary mission is to disseminate the Word of God, mainly through literature. It is one of the largest distributors of gospel tracts and leaflets in the United Kingdom, with over 100 titles and many thousands dispatched annually. In addition to Golden Bells, Hayes Press also publishes other paperbacks and eBooks, and Needed Truth magazine, a Bible teaching ministry of the Churches of God (www.churchesofgod.info).

If you would like to contact Hayes Press, there are a number of ways you can do so:

By mail: c/o The Barn, Flaxlands, Royal Wootton Bassett, Wiltshire, UK SN4 8DY

By phone: 07341 379815

By eMail: info@hayespress.org

via Facebook: www.facebook.com/hayespress.org